HEALTHY ACTIVE LIVING
Student Activity Handbook 9

We are grateful to the following individuals for their contributions to this handbook:

Sheila Allen
Havergal College

Rasa Augaitis
St Mary's Catholic Secondary School

Sarah Bruce
Havergal College

Danielle Dutchak
Robert Bateman High School

Steve Friesen
St James Catholic School

Peter Glaab
St James Catholic School

Derek Graham
Westdale Secondary School

Dave Inglis
H B Beal Secondary School

Jamie Nunn
Vice-Principal, Westmount Secondary School

Kelly Pace
St. Clement's School

Kim Parkes
Westdale Secondary School

Kari Platman
Havergal College

Kelly Stenton
Havergal College

Carolyn Temertzoglou
Havergal College/Ontario Institute for Studies in Education (OISE)

Deb Townsley
North Middlesex District High School

Michele Van Bargen
Strathroy District Collegiate Institute

HEALTHY ACTIVE LIVING
Student Activity Handbook 9

Ted Temertzoglou

Birchmount Park Collegiate Institute
Toronto District School Board

Thompson Educational Publishing, Inc.
Toronto

Information on how to obtain copies of this book may be obtained from:

Website:	http://www.thompsonbooks.com
E-mail:	publisher@thompsonbooks.com
Telephone:	(416) 766–2763
Fax:	(416) 766–0398

ISBN: 978-1-55077-151-0

Credits:

Photos on pp. 8, 30 (top left and right, fourth from top left and right, fifth from top left, bottom left and right), 48–50 by Ted Temertzoglou, Tanya Winter, and Paul Pacey, © Thompson Educational Publishing ♦ Photos used with permission of Birchmount Collegiate Institute (TDSB) on pp. 13, 17, 19, 28, 29, 35, 40, 56–58, 80, 87, 104, 107, 108 ♦ Photo on p. 106 used with permission of Northern Secondary School (TDSB) ♦ Photos used with permission of the Toronto District School Board on pp. 21, 101–102 ♦ Photo on p. 103 courtesy of the Thompson family ♦ Photo on p. 23 used with permission of A.Y. Jackson Secondary School (TDSB) ♦ Photos on pp. 15, 41, 42, 53 by Michelle Prata ♦ Photo on p. 43 used with permission of Westwood Middle School (TDSB) ♦ Photo on p. 44 used with permission of East York Collegiate Institute (TDSB) ♦ Photos on pp. 46, 61, 68, 73, 76, 83, 91–94: iStockphoto ♦ Photos on pp. 25 and 77: Shutterstock ♦ Photo on p. 51: Mount Royal College Recreation Centre, Calgary, AB ♦ Artwork and illustrations on pp. 30 (second from top left and right, third from top left and right, fifth from top right, sixth from top left and right), 31–34, 37–39, 63, 81 by Bart Vallecoccia ♦ Cigarette warning label on p. 82, source: Graphic Health Warning, http://www.hc-sc.gc.ca/hl-vs/tobac-tabac/legislation/label-etiquette/graph/citydies-villemeurt9_e.html, Health Canada, 2000. Reproduced with the permission of the Minister of Public Works and Government Services Canada, and courtesy of Health Canada, 2007.

Publisher: Keith Thompson

Managing Editor: Jennie Worden

Cover Design: Tibor Choleva

Page design, graphic art, and special effects: Tibor Choleva

Production Editor: Megan Moore Burns

Copyeditor: Crystal J. Hall

Proofreader: Katy Harrison

Senior Editor: Rachel Stuckey

Every reasonable effort has been made to acquire permission for copyrighted materials used in this book and to acknowledge such permissions accurately. Any errors or omissions called to the publisher's attention will be corrected in future printings. We acknowledge the support of the Government of Canada through the Book Publishing Industry Development Program for our publishing activities.

Printed in Canada. 1 2 3 4 5   09 08 07

Table of Contents

A Typical Physical Education Class 7

Healthy Active Living Literacy 8

Assessing Your Participation 9

Okay, You Be the Teacher 10

Using Your Daily Activity Journal 11

UNIT 1 Healthy Active Living

Textbook Scavenger Hunt 26

What Is Healthy Active Living? 27

Health-Related Fitness 28

Anatomical Position 29

Anatomical Terms 30

Human Skeleton (Anterior) 31

Human Skeleton (Posterior) 32

Major Muscles (Anterior) 33

Major Muscles (Posterior) 34

Joint Movements 35

Defining Movements at Joints 36

The Human Heart 37

The Path of Blood 38

The Respiratory System 39

Keeping Your Cardiorespiratory System Fit 40

UNIT 2 Fitness Measurements and Appraisals

KWL for Fitness Appraisals 42

Finding Your Target Heart Rate Zone 43

Using a Pedometer 44

Cardiorespiratory Appraisals 45

mCAFT 45

12-Minute Run 46

Beep Test 46

Muscular Strength and Endurance Appraisals 47

Grip Strength 47

Push-Ups 48

Partial Curl-Ups 49

Sit-and-Reach 49

Vertical Jump 50

UNIT 3 Fitness Planning, Exercises, and Injury Prevention

My Healthy Active Living Plan 53

My Healthy Active Living Action Plan 54

Assessing My Fitness Goals 55

The FITT Principle 56

Where Do I Go From Here? 57

Resistance Training Log 59

UNIT 4 Human Reproduction, Sexuality, and Intimacy

What Do I Know About Human Reproduction, Sexuality, and Intimacy? 63

Sexuality: Mix and Match 64

Sexuality: Key Terms 64

Sexuality: Concept Map 65

Ages and Stages of Development 66

Healthy Relationships 67

Sources of Pressure 69

He Said/She Said 70

Thinking Through Sexual Health Issues 71

Community Services 72

UNIT 5 Drug Use and Abuse

What Do I Know About Drugs? 75

Tobacco and Alcohol: Mix and Match 76

Marijuana, Illegal Drugs, and Steroids 76

Drugs and Their Effects 77

Continuum of Risk 78

Myths and Facts about Drug Use 79

Tobacco and Alcohol 81

Media Analysis 82

Marijuana and Other Illegal Drugs 83

Decision Making—IDEAL in Action 84

Drug Use and Abuse—Key Terms 85

School and Community Strategies to Combat Drug Abuse 86

UNIT 6 Conflict Resolution and Personal Safety

What Do I Know About Violence and Conflict?   89

Combatting Violence, Creating Safe Schools   90

Types of Conflict   91

Triggers of Anger and Anger Management   92

Types of Abuse and Violence   93

Impact of Non-Physical Abuse   94

Effects of Abuse and Violence   95

PLACEMAT: Solutions and Strategies   96

Conflict Resolution and Personal Safety— Key Terms   97

Building Safe Communities   98

UNIT 7 Nutrition for Everyday Performance

See Grade 10 Student Activity Handbook

UNIT 8 Physical Activities and Sports

Invasion/Territory Games   101

    Strategies and Tactics   101

Phases of a Skill   102

Net/Wall Games   103

    Strategies and Tactics   103

Phases of a Skill   104

Striking/Fielding Games   105

    Strategies and Tactics   105

Phases of a Skill   106

Target Games   107

    Strategies and Tactics   107

Phases of a Skill   108

Appendix ACT High School CPR Student Manual (Supplementary Material)

Parent Information and Volunteer Letter   110

Emergency Care Scenarios   111

Performance Checklist - One-Person CPR   113

Sample Performance Rubric — CPR   114

Student Evaluation of the CPR Program   115

Lifesaver Awards Program—Feedback Form   116

A Typical Physical Education Class

You are about to discover the fascinating world of Health and Physical Education and the unique way in which it will enhance your life. How many other courses, taken during your high school career, can offer you the opportunity to lead a healthier active lifestyle?

Remember that it's not your athletic ability that counts, it's the effort and commitment that you display. Your teacher will show you where you will get changed and what you are to do with your clothes. Show up to class as early as you can, changed and ready to go.

Physical education classes are usually made up of four components during each class. These are:

1. The Warm-Up (5 to 12 minutes)

The warm-up prepares the body for activity. It could include a jog/run/skip/circuit, tag, or low, organizational-type games for a set amount of time, or laps followed by a dynamic stretch component. Usually the teacher will lead the warm-up, but you might be asked to lead one in the future to assess your leadership skills.

2. Conditioning Components or Fitness Blast (10 to 20 minutes)

This usually deals with some or all of the health-related fitness components such as muscular strength, muscular endurance, cardio-vascular endurance, and flexibility. During this component you will be asked to fill in your Activity Journal in order to monitor your intensity (how hard you worked).

3. Instruction of Activity (30 to 40 minutes)

The teacher will introduce the game, sport, or activity for the day or for the unit, which may last approximately 5 to 7 days. At this point, the teacher will tell you what you will be assessed and evaluated on. Pay close attention to what he or she says; after all, this is what your mark will be based on.

4. The Cool-Down (5 to 7 minutes)

The purpose of the cool-down is to return your body to resting levels. It consists of light aerobic activity followed by a static stretch. The cool-down helps the body get rid of waste materials such as lactic acid, which can harm the body if produced in large amounts.

Healthy Active Living Literacy

Throughout the year, you will learn new words, or terminology, that describe what it means to be healthy and active. Create your own personal list of words and their definitions in the rectangles below.

Glossary of Key Terms

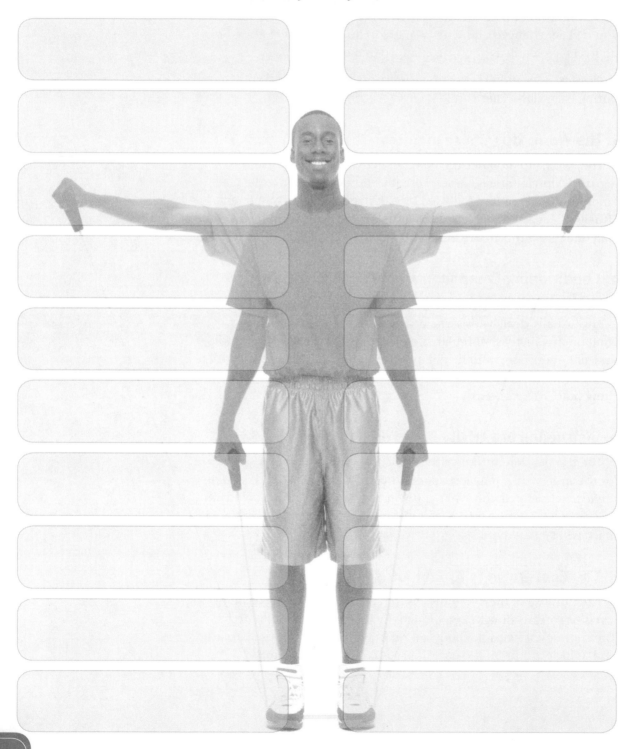

Assessing Your Participation

The surest way to achieve a high mark in health and physical education is to participate fully and safely, and respect your classmates and your school. Three key areas that you will be assessed and evaluated on this year are listed in the rubric below.

Category	Criteria	Level 1	Level 2	Level 3	Level 4
Participation	Demonstrates effort in activities and stays on task Is ready to participate and take part Demonstrates a determined effort	Infrequently participates actively	Sometimes participates actively	Regularly participates actively	Always or almost always participates actively
Safety	Demonstrates safe and correct use of equipment and procedures	Uses procedures and equipment safely and correctly only with supervision	Uses procedures and equipment safely and correctly with some supervision	Uses procedures and equipment safely and correctly	Demonstrates and promotes the correct use of procedures and equipment
Social	Demonstrates appropriate behaviour (e.g., cooperation, respect, fair play) Works well with others	Infrequently demonstrates appropriate behaviour	Sometimes demonstrates appropriate behaviour	Regularly demonstrates appropriate behaviour	Always or almost always demonstrates appropriate behaviour

Okay, You Be the Teacher

You now get your wish—to become the teacher. Read the three case studies below and use the participation rubric on page 9 to assess these three students.

Case 1: Tibor

Tibor has forgotten his required gym uniform four times and, when he brought it the other two times, he arrived late. He does not get along with the other students because he always wants things to go his way. He has yet to show maximal effort in class, and usually puts others down that do. You have spoken to him several times but Tibor has yet to change his attitude.

Level _____

What advice would you offer Tibor?

_____
_____
_____
_____
_____

Case 2: Marella

Marella is always in the required uniform and participates all the time while encouraging others to do the same. She usually arrives early and begins jogging or walking a couple of laps before class begins. When someone calls for the attention of the class, Marella is one of the first to follow the request of the teacher or whoever is leading the class. She is not the most athletically gifted student, but few work harder than her. She enjoys being active and likes the results of leading a healthy active lifestyle.

Level _____

What advice would you offer Marella?

_____
_____
_____
_____
_____

Case 3: Amin

Amin is the most talented athlete in the class, but he finds it hard to pay attention to the teacher or other students giving instruction. He usually has his required gym uniform and regularly demonstrates a determined effort. When the teacher introduces a new game, Amin usually interrupts, saying that he only wants to play floor hockey. He does not see the benefit in running around the track or the gym for twelve minutes, or in push-ups, sit-ups, or flexibility work in class.

Level _____

What advice would you offer Amin?

_____
_____
_____
_____
_____

Using Your Daily Activity Journal

Monitoring your daily activity, both in school and out, is an excellent way to track your progress. In fact, successful people in many aspects of life do this on a regular basis. Below is a detailed explanation on how to use your activity journal, including a sample week.

After each day, reflect on the physical activity you have participated in and record it in your activity journal. If the activity was done during Health & Physical Education (H&PE) class, assess your participation, safety, and social skills. Refer to the rubric on page 9 for the criteria of each level. Be sure to use the symbols provided to describe your physical activity.

At the end of the month, you will have a very good snapshot of your monthly physical activity. Be sure to record your heart rate and total step count when appropriate.

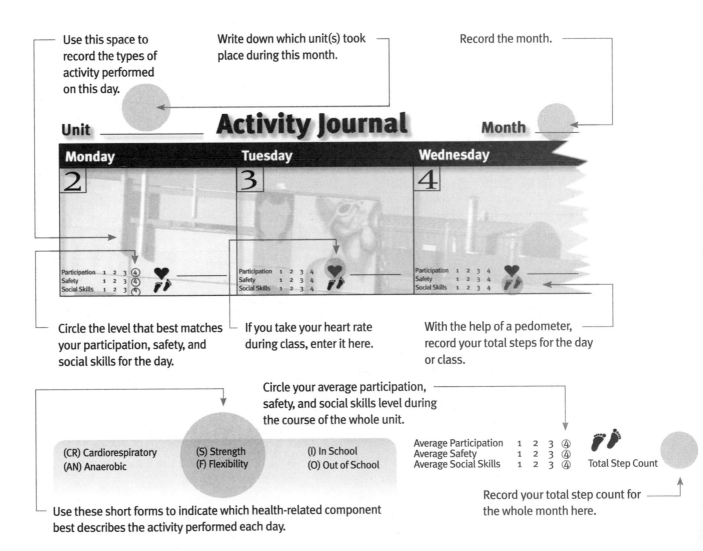

Use this space to record the types of activity performed on this day.

Write down which unit(s) took place during this month.

Record the month.

Activity Journal

Unit _____   Month _____

Monday 2	Tuesday 3	Wednesday 4

Participation 1 2 3 ④
Safety 1 2 3 ④
Social Skills 1 2 3 ④

Participation 1 2 3 4
Safety 1 2 3 4
Social Skills 1 2 3 4

Participation 1 2 3 4
Safety 1 2 3 4
Social Skills 1 2 3 4

Circle the level that best matches your participation, safety, and social skills for the day.

If you take your heart rate during class, enter it here.

With the help of a pedometer, record your total steps for the day or class.

Circle your average participation, safety, and social skills level during the course of the whole unit.

(CR) Cardiorespiratory   (S) Strength   (I) In School
(AN) Anaerobic   (F) Flexibility (O) Out of School

Average Participation   1 2 3 ④
Average Safety   1 2 3 ④
Average Social Skills   1 2 3 ④   Total Step Count

Record your total step count for the whole month here.

Use these short forms to indicate which health-related component best describes the activity performed each day.

Activity Journal

Unit _____

Month _____

Monday	Tuesday	Wednesday	Thursday	Friday	Saturday/Sunday

Row 1:

Monday: Participation 1 2 3 4 / Safety 1 2 3 4 / Social Skills 1 2 3 4

Wednesday: Participation 1 2 3 4 / Safety 1 2 3 4 / Social Skills 1 2 3 4

Friday: Participation 1 2 3 4 / Safety 1 2 3 4 / Social Skills 1 2 3 4

Row 2:

Monday: Participation 1 2 3 4 / Safety 1 2 3 4 / Social Skills 1 2 3 4

Tuesday: Participation 1 2 3 4 / Safety 1 2 3 4 / Social Skills 1 2 3 4

Thursday: Participation 1 2 3 4 / Safety 1 2 3 4 / Social Skills 1 2 3 4

Friday: Participation 1 2 3 4 / Safety 1 2 3 4 / Social Skills 1 2 3 4

Row 3:

Monday: Participation 1 2 3 4 / Safety 1 2 3 4 / Social Skills 1 2 3 4

Tuesday: Participation 1 2 3 4 / Safety 1 2 3 4 / Social Skills 1 2 3 4

Thursday: Participation 1 2 3 4 / Safety 1 2 3 4 / Social Skills 1 2 3 4

Friday: Participation 1 2 3 4 / Safety 1 2 3 4 / Social Skills 1 2 3 4

Row 4:

Monday: Participation 1 2 3 4 / Safety 1 2 3 4 / Social Skills 1 2 3 4

Tuesday: Participation 1 2 3 4 / Safety 1 2 3 4 / Social Skills 1 2 3 4

Thursday: Participation 1 2 3 4 / Safety 1 2 3 4 / Social Skills 1 2 3 4

Friday: Participation 1 2 3 4 / Safety 1 2 3 4 / Social Skills 1 2 3 4

Row 5:

Monday: Participation 1 2 3 4 / Safety 1 2 3 4 / Social Skills 1 2 3 4

Tuesday: Participation 1 2 3 4 / Safety 1 2 3 4 / Social Skills 1 2 3 4

Wednesday: Participation 1 2 3 4 / Safety 1 2 3 4 / Social Skills 1 2 3 4

Thursday: Participation 1 2 3 4 / Safety 1 2 3 4 / Social Skills 1 2 3 4

Friday: Participation 1 2 3 4 / Safety 1 2 3 4 / Social Skills 1 2 3 4

(CR) Cardiorespiratory
(AN) Anaerobic

(S) Strength
(F) Flexibility

(I) In School
(O) Out of School

Average Participation 1 2 3 4
Average Safety 1 2 3 4
Average Social Skills 1 2 3 4

👣 Total Step Count _____

Healthy Active Living — Student Activity Handbook
© Copyright. It is illegal to photocopy without permission.

PFP

Activity Journal Questions

Once you have finished your monthly recordings, complete the sentence stems below. This will allow you to reflect on your successes and the challenges you have faced so far.

1. The area of fitness I improved upon the most was ...

_____

_____

_____

_____

_____

_____

2. An area of fitness I can improve on is ...

_____

_____

3. Something I found challenging during this unit(s) was ...

_____

_____

_____

_____

_____

4. During this unit(s), I was most proud of myself when ...

_____

_____

5. Reflecting back on this unit(s), I would give myself the following level based on my overall participation (refer to page 9 to review the criteria for each level and circle the appropriate one):

Participation: 1   2   3   4

Safety: 1   2   3   4

Social Skills: 1   2   3   4

PFP

Activity Journal

Unit _____   Month _____

Monday	Tuesday	Wednesday	Thursday	Friday	Saturday/Sunday
Participation 1 2 3 4 Safety 1 2 3 4 Social Skills 1 2 3 4	Participation 1 2 3 4 Safety 1 2 3 4 Social Skills 1 2 3 4	Participation 1 2 3 4 Safety 1 2 3 4 Social Skills 1 2 3 4	Participation 1 2 3 4 Safety 1 2 3 4 Social Skills 1 2 3 4	Participation 1 2 3 4 Safety 1 2 3 4 Social Skills 1 2 3 4	
Participation 1 2 3 4 Safety 1 2 3 4 Social Skills 1 2 3 4	Participation 1 2 3 4 Safety 1 2 3 4 Social Skills 1 2 3 4	Participation 1 2 3 4 Safety 1 2 3 4 Social Skills 1 2 3 4	Participation 1 2 3 4 Safety 1 2 3 4 Social Skills 1 2 3 4	Participation 1 2 3 4 Safety 1 2 3 4 Social Skills 1 2 3 4	
Participation 1 2 3 4 Safety 1 2 3 4 Social Skills 1 2 3 4	Participation 1 2 3 4 Safety 1 2 3 4 Social Skills 1 2 3 4	Participation 1 2 3 4 Safety 1 2 3 4 Social Skills 1 2 3 4	Participation 1 2 3 4 Safety 1 2 3 4 Social Skills 1 2 3 4	Participation 1 2 3 4 Safety 1 2 3 4 Social Skills 1 2 3 4	
Participation 1 2 3 4 Safety 1 2 3 4 Social Skills 1 2 3 4	Participation 1 2 3 4 Safety 1 2 3 4 Social Skills 1 2 3 4	Participation 1 2 3 4 Safety 1 2 3 4 Social Skills 1 2 3 4	Participation 1 2 3 4 Safety 1 2 3 4 Social Skills 1 2 3 4	Participation 1 2 3 4 Safety 1 2 3 4 Social Skills 1 2 3 4	
Participation 1 2 3 4 Safety 1 2 3 4 Social Skills 1 2 3 4	Participation 1 2 3 4 Safety 1 2 3 4 Social Skills 1 2 3 4	Participation 1 2 3 4 Safety 1 2 3 4 Social Skills 1 2 3 4	Participation 1 2 3 4 Safety 1 2 3 4 Social Skills 1 2 3 4	Participation 1 2 3 4 Safety 1 2 3 4 Social Skills 1 2 3 4	

(CR) Cardiorespiratory   (S) Strength   (I) In School
(AN) Anaerobic   (F) Flexibility   (O) Out of School

Average Participation   1 2 3 4
Average Safety   1 2 3 4
Average Social Skills   1 2 3 4

Total Step Count _____

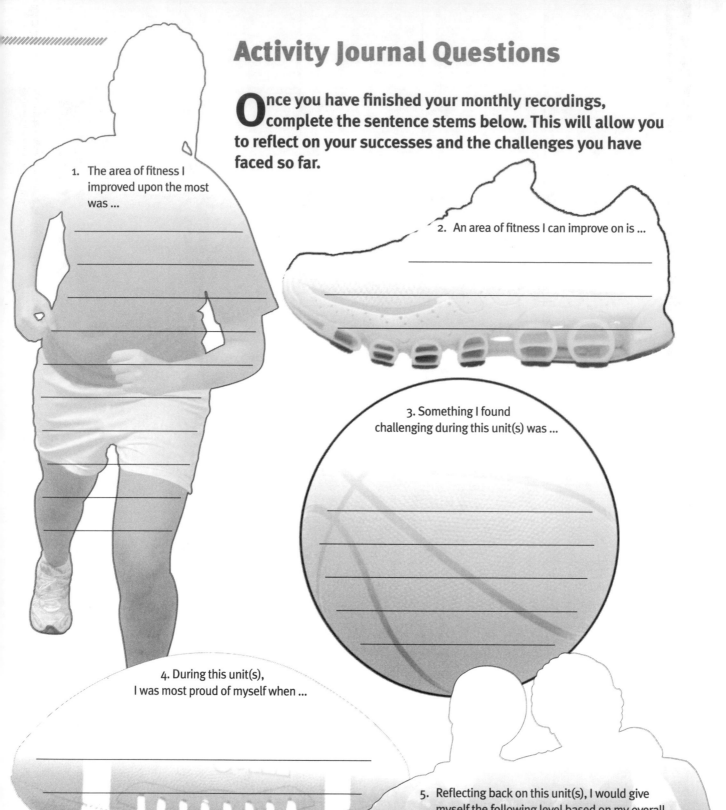

Activity Journal Questions

Once you have finished your monthly recordings, complete the sentence stems below. This will allow you to reflect on your successes and the challenges you have faced so far.

1. The area of fitness I improved upon the most was ...

_____

_____

_____

_____

_____

_____

_____

2. An area of fitness I can improve on is ...

_____

_____

_____

3. Something I found challenging during this unit(s) was ...

_____

_____

_____

_____

4. During this unit(s), I was most proud of myself when ...

_____

_____

_____

5. Reflecting back on this unit(s), I would give myself the following level based on my overall participation (refer to page 9 to review the criteria for each level and circle the appropriate one):

Participation: 1   2   3   4

Safety: 1   2   3   4

Social Skills: 1   2   3   4

PFP

Unit ______________________

Activity Journal

Month ______________________

Monday	Tuesday	Wednesday	Thursday	Friday	Saturday/Sunday
Participation 1 2 3 4 Safety 1 2 3 4 Social Skills 1 2 3 4 ______	Participation 1 2 3 4 Safety 1 2 3 4 Social Skills 1 2 3 4 ______	Participation 1 2 3 4 Safety 1 2 3 4 Social Skills 1 2 3 4 ______	Participation 1 2 3 4 Safety 1 2 3 4 Social Skills 1 2 3 4 ______	Participation 1 2 3 4 Safety 1 2 3 4 Social Skills 1 2 3 4 ______	______
Participation 1 2 3 4 Safety 1 2 3 4 Social Skills 1 2 3 4 ______	Participation 1 2 3 4 Safety 1 2 3 4 Social Skills 1 2 3 4 ______	Participation 1 2 3 4 Safety 1 2 3 4 Social Skills 1 2 3 4 ______	Participation 1 2 3 4 Safety 1 2 3 4 Social Skills 1 2 3 4 ______	Participation 1 2 3 4 Safety 1 2 3 4 Social Skills 1 2 3 4 ______	______
Participation 1 2 3 4 Safety 1 2 3 4 Social Skills 1 2 3 4 ______	Participation 1 2 3 4 Safety 1 2 3 4 Social Skills 1 2 3 4 ______	Participation 1 2 3 4 Safety 1 2 3 4 Social Skills 1 2 3 4 ______	Participation 1 2 3 4 Safety 1 2 3 4 Social Skills 1 2 3 4 ______	Participation 1 2 3 4 Safety 1 2 3 4 Social Skills 1 2 3 4 ______	______
Participation 1 2 3 4 Safety 1 2 3 4 Social Skills 1 2 3 4 ______	Participation 1 2 3 4 Safety 1 2 3 4 Social Skills 1 2 3 4 ______	Participation 1 2 3 4 Safety 1 2 3 4 Social Skills 1 2 3 4 ______	Participation 1 2 3 4 Safety 1 2 3 4 Social Skills 1 2 3 4 ______	Participation 1 2 3 4 Safety 1 2 3 4 Social Skills 1 2 3 4 ______	______
Participation 1 2 3 4 Safety 1 2 3 4 Social Skills 1 2 3 4 ______	Participation 1 2 3 4 Safety 1 2 3 4 Social Skills 1 2 3 4 ______	Participation 1 2 3 4 Safety 1 2 3 4 Social Skills 1 2 3 4 ______	Participation 1 2 3 4 Safety 1 2 3 4 Social Skills 1 2 3 4 ______	Participation 1 2 3 4 Safety 1 2 3 4 Social Skills 1 2 3 4 ______	______

(CR) Cardiorespiratory
(AN) Anaerobic

(S) Strength
(F) Flexibility

(I) In School
(O) Out of School

Average Participation 1 2 3 4
Average Safety 1 2 3 4
Average Social Skills 1 2 3 4

Total Step Count ______

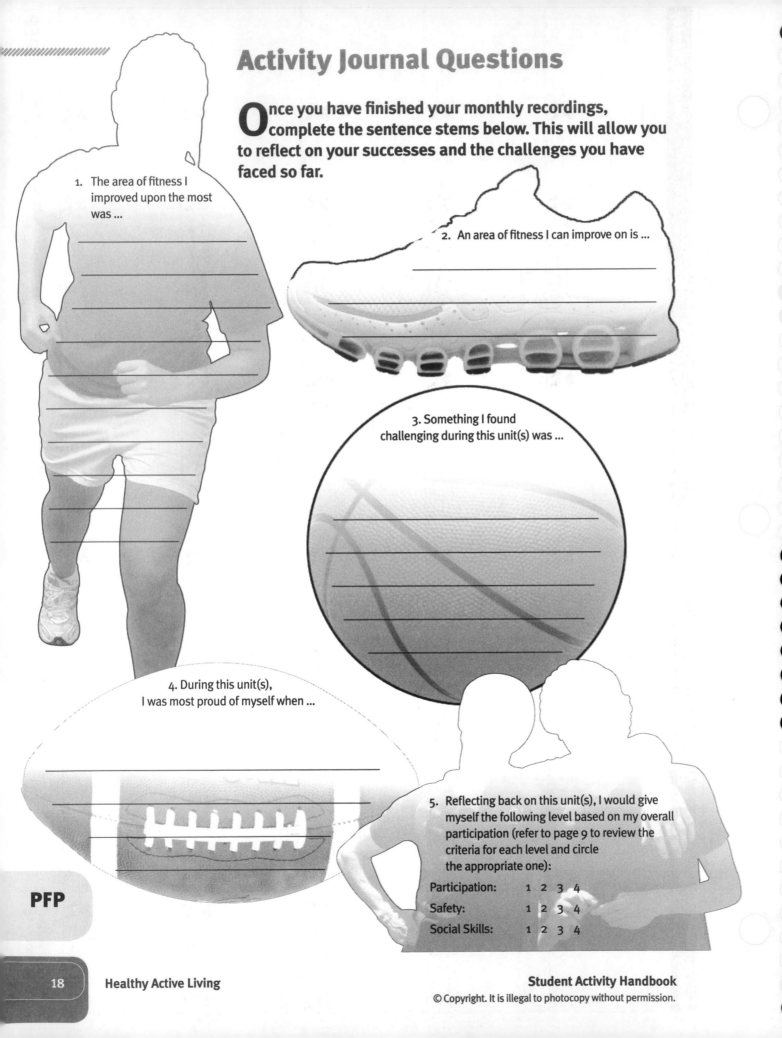

Activity Journal Questions

Once you have finished your monthly recordings, complete the sentence stems below. This will allow you to reflect on your successes and the challenges you have faced so far.

1. The area of fitness I improved upon the most was ...

_____

_____

_____

_____

_____

_____

_____

2. An area of fitness I can improve on is ...

_____

_____

3. Something I found challenging during this unit(s) was ...

_____

_____

_____

_____

_____

4. During this unit(s), I was most proud of myself when ...

_____

_____

_____

5. Reflecting back on this unit(s), I would give myself the following level based on my overall participation (refer to page 9 to review the criteria for each level and circle the appropriate one):

Participation: 1 2 3 4

Safety: 1 2 3 4

Social Skills: 1 2 3 4

PFP

Student Activity Handbook

Activity Journal

Unit _____   Month _____

Monday	Tuesday	Wednesday	Thursday	Friday	Saturday/Sunday
Participation 1 2 3 4 Safety 1 2 3 4 Social Skills 1 2 3 4	Participation 1 2 3 4 Safety 1 2 3 4 Social Skills 1 2 3 4	Participation 1 2 3 4 Safety 1 2 3 4 Social Skills 1 2 3 4	Participation 1 2 3 4 Safety 1 2 3 4 Social Skills 1 2 3 4	Participation 1 2 3 4 Safety 1 2 3 4 Social Skills 1 2 3 4	
Participation 1 2 3 4 Safety 1 2 3 4 Social Skills 1 2 3 4	Participation 1 2 3 4 Safety 1 2 3 4 Social Skills 1 2 3 4	Participation 1 2 3 4 Safety 1 2 3 4 Social Skills 1 2 3 4	Participation 1 2 3 4 Safety 1 2 3 4 Social Skills 1 2 3 4	Participation 1 2 3 4 Safety 1 2 3 4 Social Skills 1 2 3 4	
Participation 1 2 3 4 Safety 1 2 3 4 Social Skills 1 2 3 4	Participation 1 2 3 4 Safety 1 2 3 4 Social Skills 1 2 3 4	Participation 1 2 3 4 Safety 1 2 3 4 Social Skills 1 2 3 4	Participation 1 2 3 4 Safety 1 2 3 4 Social Skills 1 2 3 4	Participation 1 2 3 4 Safety 1 2 3 4 Social Skills 1 2 3 4	
Participation 1 2 3 4 Safety 1 2 3 4 Social Skills 1 2 3 4	Participation 1 2 3 4 Safety 1 2 3 4 Social Skills 1 2 3 4	Participation 1 2 3 4 Safety 1 2 3 4 Social Skills 1 2 3 4	Participation 1 2 3 4 Safety 1 2 3 4 Social Skills 1 2 3 4	Participation 1 2 3 4 Safety 1 2 3 4 Social Skills 1 2 3 4	
Participation 1 2 3 4 Safety 1 2 3 4 Social Skills 1 2 3 4	Participation 1 2 3 4 Safety 1 2 3 4 Social Skills 1 2 3 4	Participation 1 2 3 4 Safety 1 2 3 4 Social Skills 1 2 3 4	Participation 1 2 3 4 Safety 1 2 3 4 Social Skills 1 2 3 4	Participation 1 2 3 4 Safety 1 2 3 4 Social Skills 1 2 3 4	

Average Participation 1 2 3 4
Average Safety 1 2 3 4
Average Social Skills 1 2 3 4

Total Step Count _____

(CR) Cardiorespiratory
(AN) Anaerobic

(S) Strength
(F) Flexibility

(I) In School
(O) Out of School

Healthy Active Living — Student Activity Handbook

PFP

Activity Journal Questions

Once you have finished your monthly recordings, complete the sentence stems below. This will allow you to reflect on your successes and the challenges you have faced so far.

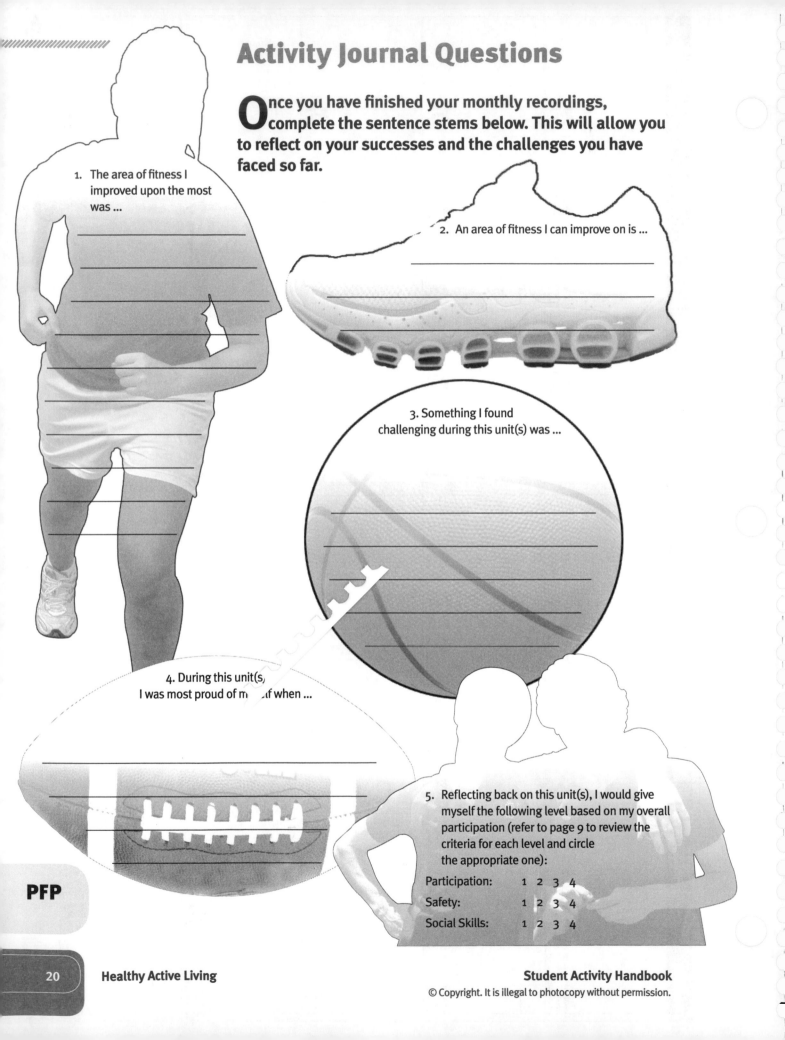

1. The area of fitness I improved upon the most was ...

_____

_____

_____

_____

_____

_____

_____

2. An area of fitness I can improve on is ...

_____

_____

3. Something I found challenging during this unit(s) was ...

_____

_____

_____

_____

_____

4. During this unit(s) I was most proud of myself when ...

_____

_____

_____

5. Reflecting back on this unit(s), I would give myself the following level based on my overall participation (refer to page 9 to review the criteria for each level and circle the appropriate one):

Participation: 1 2 3 4

Safety: 1 2 3 4

Social Skills: 1 2 3 4

PFP

Activity Journal

Unit _____ Month _____

Monday	Tuesday	Wednesday	Thursday	Friday	Saturday/Sunday
Participation 1 2 3 4 Safety 1 2 3 4 Social Skills 1 2 3 4	Participation 1 2 3 4 Safety 1 2 3 4 Social Skills 1 2 3 4	Participation 1 2 3 4 Safety 1 2 3 4 Social Skills 1 2 3 4	Participation 1 2 3 4 Safety 1 2 3 4 Social Skills 1 2 3 4	Participation 1 2 3 4 Safety 1 2 3 4 Social Skills 1 2 3 4	
Participation 1 2 3 4 Safety 1 2 3 4 Social Skills 1 2 3 4	Participation 1 2 3 4 Safety 1 2 3 4 Social Skills 1 2 3 4	Participation 1 2 3 4 Safety 1 2 3 4 Social Skills 1 2 3 4	Participation 1 2 3 4 Safety 1 2 3 4 Social Skills 1 2 3 4	Participation 1 2 3 4 Safety 1 2 3 4 Social Skills 1 2 3 4	
Participation 1 2 3 4 Safety 1 2 3 4 Social Skills 1 2 3 4	Participation 1 2 3 4 Safety 1 2 3 4 Social Skills 1 2 3 4	Participation 1 2 3 4 Safety 1 2 3 4 Social Skills 1 2 3 4	Participation 1 2 3 4 Safety 1 2 3 4 Social Skills 1 2 3 4	Participation 1 2 3 4 Safety 1 2 3 4 Social Skills 1 2 3 4	
Participation 1 2 3 4 Safety 1 2 3 4 Social Skills 1 2 3 4	Participation 1 2 3 4 Safety 1 2 3 4 Social Skills 1 2 3 4	Participation 1 2 3 4 Safety 1 2 3 4 Social Skills 1 2 3 4	Participation 1 2 3 4 Safety 1 2 3 4 Social Skills 1 2 3 4	Participation 1 2 3 4 Safety 1 2 3 4 Social Skills 1 2 3 4	
Participation 1 2 3 4 Safety 1 2 3 4 Social Skills 1 2 3 4	Participation 1 2 3 4 Safety 1 2 3 4 Social Skills 1 2 3 4	Participation 1 2 3 4 Safety 1 2 3 4 Social Skills 1 2 3 4	Participation 1 2 3 4 Safety 1 2 3 4 Social Skills 1 2 3 4	Participation 1 2 3 4 Safety 1 2 3 4 Social Skills 1 2 3 4	

(CR) Cardiorespiratory
(AN) Anaerobic
(S) Strength
(F) Flexibility
(I) In School
(O) Out of School

Average Participation 1 2 3 4
Average Safety 1 2 3 4
Average Social Skills 1 2 3 4

Total Step Count _____

Activity Journal Questions

Once you have finished your monthly recordings, complete the sentence stems below. This will allow you to reflect on your successes and the challenges you have faced so far.

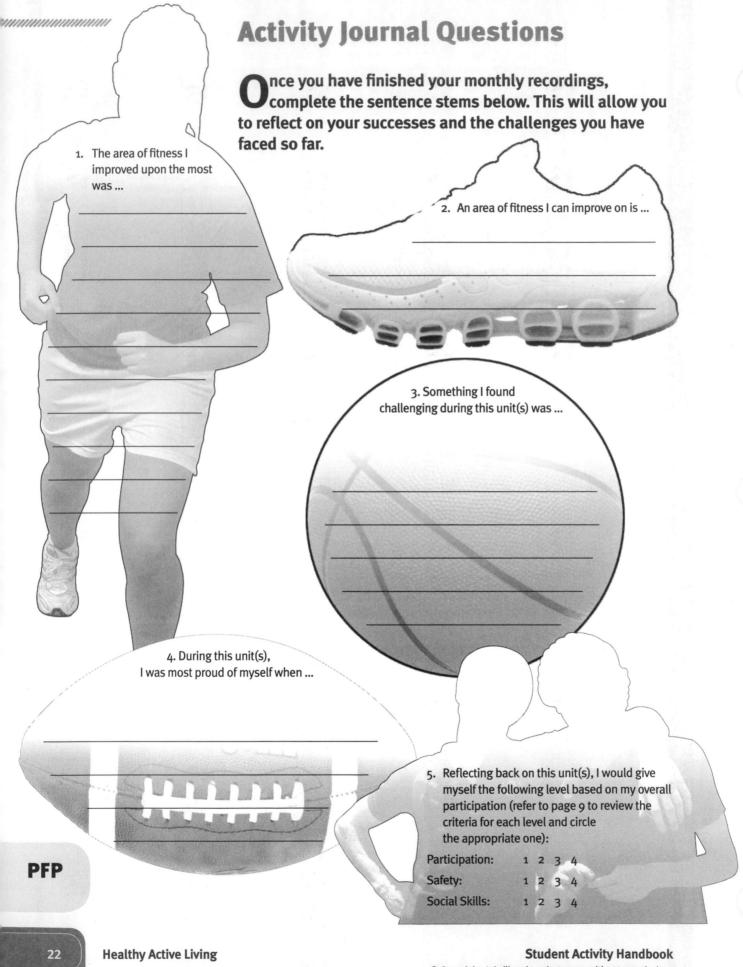

1. The area of fitness I improved upon the most was ...

_____

_____

_____

_____

_____

_____

_____

2. An area of fitness I can improve on is ...

_____

_____

3. Something I found challenging during this unit(s) was ...

_____

_____

_____

_____

_____

4. During this unit(s), I was most proud of myself when ...

_____

_____

_____

5. Reflecting back on this unit(s), I would give myself the following level based on my overall participation (refer to page 9 to review the criteria for each level and circle the appropriate one):

Participation: 1   2   3   4

Safety: 1   2   3   4

Social Skills: 1   2   3   4

PFP

Activity Journal

Unit _____   Month _____

Monday	Tuesday	Wednesday	Thursday	Friday	Saturday/Sunday
Participation 1 2 3 4 Safety 1 2 3 4 Social Skills 1 2 3 4	Participation 1 2 3 4 Safety 1 2 3 4 Social Skills 1 2 3 4	Participation 1 2 3 4 Safety 1 2 3 4 Social Skills 1 2 3 4	Participation 1 2 3 4 Safety 1 2 3 4 Social Skills 1 2 3 4	Participation 1 2 3 4 Safety 1 2 3 4 Social Skills 1 2 3 4	
Participation 1 2 3 4 Safety 1 2 3 4 Social Skills 1 2 3 4	Participation 1 2 3 4 Safety 1 2 3 4 Social Skills 1 2 3 4	Participation 1 2 3 4 Safety 1 2 3 4 Social Skills 1 2 3 4	Participation 1 2 3 4 Safety 1 2 3 4 Social Skills 1 2 3 4	Participation 1 2 3 4 Safety 1 2 3 4 Social Skills 1 2 3 4	
Participation 1 2 3 4 Safety 1 2 3 4 Social Skills 1 2 3 4	Participation 1 2 3 4 Safety 1 2 3 4 Social Skills 1 2 3 4	Participation 1 2 3 4 Safety 1 2 3 4 Social Skills 1 2 3 4	Participation 1 2 3 4 Safety 1 2 3 4 Social Skills 1 2 3 4	Participation 1 2 3 4 Safety 1 2 3 4 Social Skills 1 2 3 4	
Participation 1 2 3 4 Safety 1 2 3 4 Social Skills 1 2 3 4	Participation 1 2 3 4 Safety 1 2 3 4 Social Skills 1 2 3 4	Participation 1 2 3 4 Safety 1 2 3 4 Social Skills 1 2 3 4	Participation 1 2 3 4 Safety 1 2 3 4 Social Skills 1 2 3 4	Participation 1 2 3 4 Safety 1 2 3 4 Social Skills 1 2 3 4	
Participation 1 2 3 4 Safety 1 2 3 4 Social Skills 1 2 3 4	Participation 1 2 3 4 Safety 1 2 3 4 Social Skills 1 2 3 4	Participation 1 2 3 4 Safety 1 2 3 4 Social Skills 1 2 3 4	Participation 1 2 3 4 Safety 1 2 3 4 Social Skills 1 2 3 4	Participation 1 2 3 4 Safety 1 2 3 4 Social Skills 1 2 3 4	

(CR) Cardiorespiratory   (S) Strength   (I) In School
(AN) Anaerobic   (F) Flexibility   (O) Out of School

Average Participation 1 2 3 4
Average Safety 1 2 3 4
Average Social Skills 1 2 3 4   Total Step Count _____

PFP

Activity Journal Questions

Once you have finished your monthly recordings, complete the sentence stems below. This will allow you to reflect on your successes and the challenges you have faced so far.

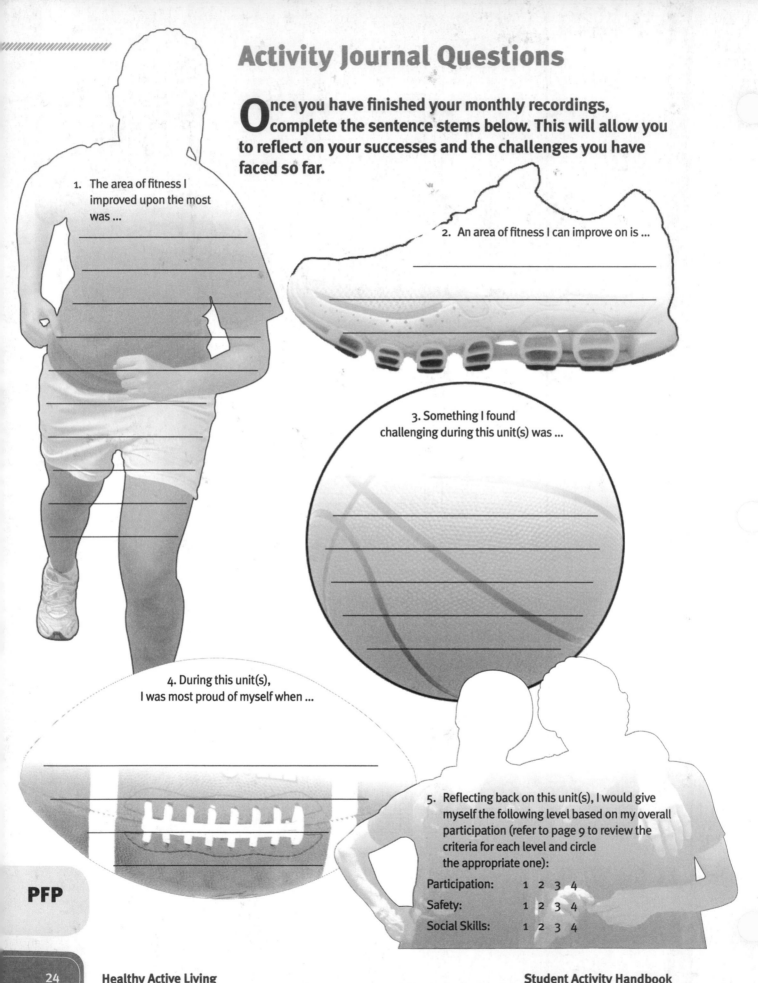

1. The area of fitness I improved upon the most was …

_____

_____

_____

_____

_____

_____

_____

2. An area of fitness I can improve on is …

_____

_____

3. Something I found challenging during this unit(s) was …

_____

_____

_____

_____

_____

4. During this unit(s), I was most proud of myself when …

_____

_____

_____

5. Reflecting back on this unit(s), I would give myself the following level based on my overall participation (refer to page 9 to review the criteria for each level and circle the appropriate one):

Participation: 1 2 3 4

Safety: 1 2 3 4

Social Skills: 1 2 3 4

PFP

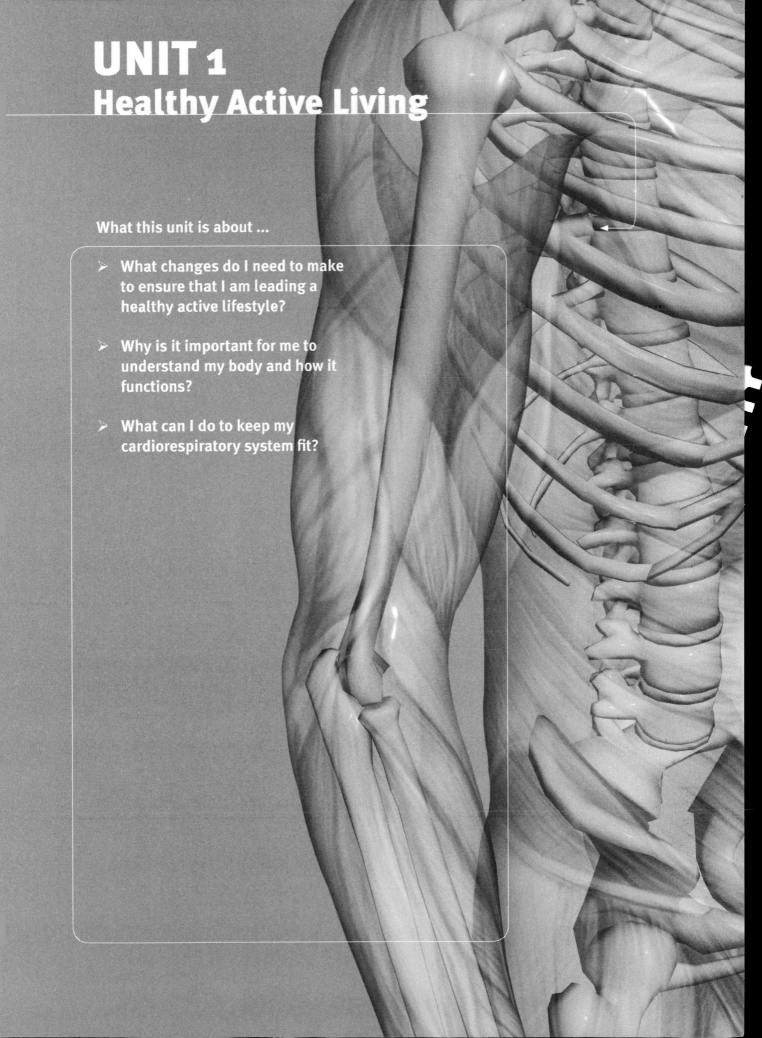

UNIT 1
Healthy Active Living

What this unit is about ...

➢ **What changes do I need to make to ensure that I am leading a healthy active lifestyle?**

➢ **Why is it important for me to understand my body and how it functions?**

➢ **What can I do to keep my cardiorespiratory system fit?**

Textbook Scavenger Hunt

Here is a chance to put your detective skills to work. This "scavenger hunt" will help you identify key elements, features, and information in your Healthy Active Living textbook.

Mission: Use your textbook to find the answers to the following questions.

1. Using the Table of Contents page, find the chapter number for the topic Caring for the Reproductive System.

2. On what page can you find information on decision-making skills?

3. What is the quote found on page 56 of Cardiorespiratory Appraisals?

4. On what page in the Key Terms would you find the term Target Heart Rate Zone?

5. What musculoskeletal fitness appraisal is covered on page 78?

6. What information is provided at the end of each chapter along with a chapter review?

7. What chapter in the textbook contains information about Conflict Resolution and Anger Management?

8. What information can be found in Appendix 1?

9. How many objectives are listed for Chapter 11 ?

10. How many major headings appear under Chapter 13?

11. How many key terms are listed in Chapter 15 and what colour are they in the text?

12. What exercises are covered on pages 122–123? What major muscle do these exercises target?

13. What Feature story is covered on page 369?

14. List the target games covered in Chapter 24.

What Is Healthy Active Living?

Before starting off on a journey, you need to know what your starting point is. This exercise will help you and your teacher learn what general knowledge you already have regarding Healthy Active Living.

Mission: Read the questions below and record your answers in the space provided.

Student name:

_____

Class/Period:

Date:

Assessed by:

Teacher ☐

Peer ☐

Self ☐

1. To me, wellness means:

_____

_____

_____

_____

4. To me, healthy eating means:

_____

_____

_____

_____

2. To me, fitness is:

_____

_____

_____

_____

5. My attitude toward physical fitness is shaped by:

_____

_____

_____

_____

3. To me, active living means:

_____

_____

_____

_____

6. I like taking part in physical activities that :

_____

_____

_____

_____

PFP

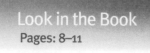
Health-Related Fitness

If you are generally "health fit," then you can probably look forward to a long life—all the important body parts (heart, lungs, muscles, bones) are in good working order and are exercised regularly.

Mission: Place the appropriate letter from column "B" into the answer box for column "A." Each answer may only be used once.

COLUMN A	ANSWER	COLUMN B
1. Cardiorespiratory		**A.** Ability to apply maximal effort in a short time
2. Agility		**B.** Ability to avoid falling over
3. Flexibility		**C.** Ability to lift a heavy weight
4. Speed		**D.** A combination of balance and agility
5. Muscular strength		**E.** Ability of the heart and lungs to deliver oxygen
6. Reaction time		**F.** Ability to change direction rapidly and accurately
7. Muscular endurance		**G.** Ability of muscle to stretch
8. Coordination		**H.** Ability to respond to a situation in a short period of time
9. Power		**I.** Ability to cover a short distance as quickly as possible
10. Balance		**J.** Ability of muscles to work over a long period of time

PFP

Exercise 1.2

Anatomical Position

The anatomical position is a universally accepted starting point for describing body parts and body movement.

Mission: Draw arrows to label the diagram below using the terms on the right-hand side of this page.

Student name:

Class/Period:

Date:

Assessed by:

Teacher ☐

Peer ☐

Self ☐

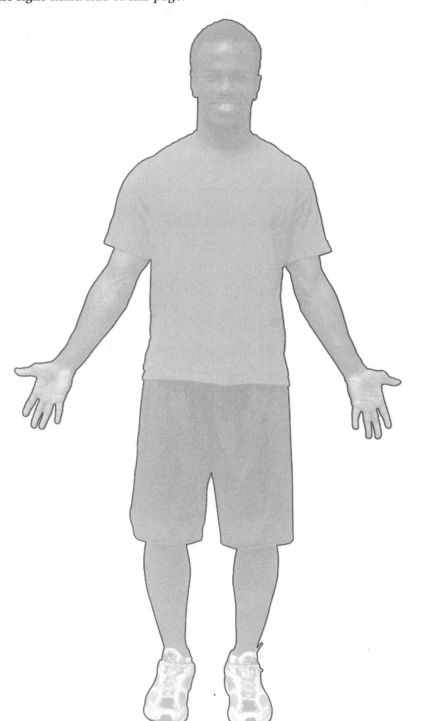

☐ midline
☐ proximal
☐ posterior
☐ superior
☐ medial
☐ distal
☐ anterior
☐ inferior
☐ lateral

Anatomical Terms

Anatomical terms are used to describe locations and relationships of body parts, starting from the anatomical position.

Mission: Place the anatomical terms below into the sentences that best describe their meaning.

superior   distal   inferior   anterior

posterior   medial   lateral

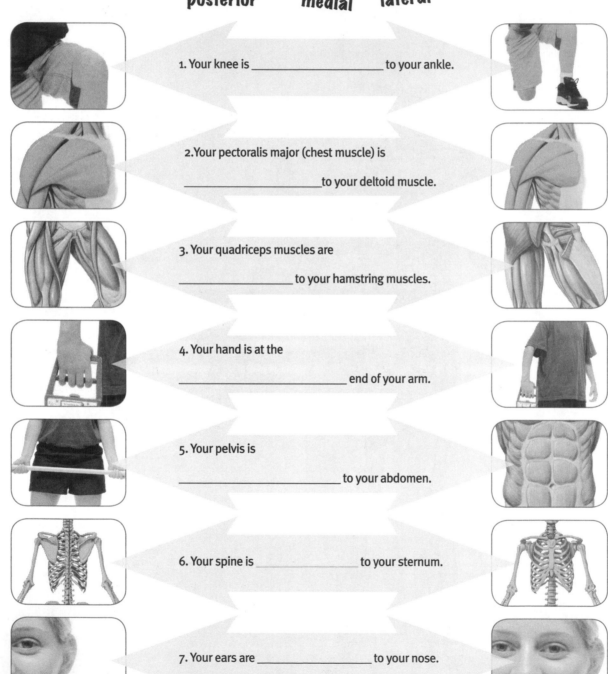

1. Your knee is _____ to your ankle.

2. Your pectoralis major (chest muscle) is _____ to your deltoid muscle.

3. Your quadriceps muscles are _____ to your hamstring muscles.

4. Your hand is at the _____ end of your arm.

5. Your pelvis is _____ to your abdomen.

6. Your spine is _____ to your sternum.

7. Your ears are _____ to your nose.

Exercise 1.3

Human Skeleton (Anterior)

Look in the Book
Pages: 24–25

This exercise will help you become more familiar with the names of the major bones.

Mission: Use a different coloured pencil crayon to colour each word on the right-hand side of the page. Then use the same colour to identify the corresponding bone on the anterior skeleton below.

Student name:

Class/Period:

Date:

Assessed by:

Teacher ☐

Peer ☐

Self ☐

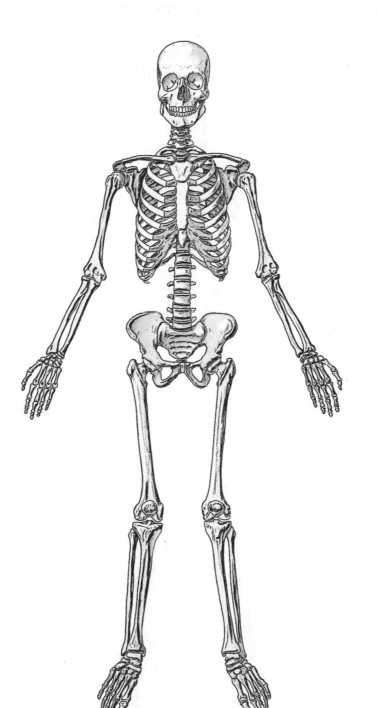

☐ Mandible
☐ Clavicle
☐ Scapula
☐ Sternum
☐ Humerus
☐ Radius
☐ Ulna
☐ Sacrum
☐ Carpals
☐ Metacarpals
☐ Phalanges
☐ Patella
☐ Xiphoid Process
☐ Ribs
☐ Femur
☐ Tibia
☐ Fibula
☐ Metatarsals

Human Skeleton (Posterior)

Mission: Use a different coloured pencil crayon to colour each word on the left-hand side of the page. Use the same colour to identify the corresponding bone on the posterior skeleton below.

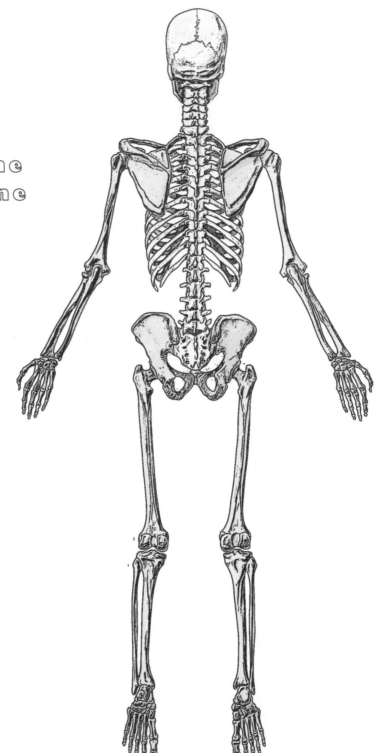

☐ Cervical Spine
☐ Thoracic Spine
☐ Lumbar
☐ Sacrum
☐ Fibula
☐ Tibia
☐ Scapula
☐ Humerus
☐ Ulna
☐ Radius
☐ Coccyx
☐ Femur
☐ Calcaneus

Exercise 1.4

Major Muscles (Anterior)

Look in the Book
Pages: 30–31

This exercise will help you become more familiar with the major muscles of the human body.

Mission: Use a different coloured pencil crayon to colour each word on the right-hand side of the page. Then use the same colour to identify the corresponding muscle on the illustration of the anterior muscular system below.

Student name:

Class/Period:

Date:

Assessed by:

Teacher ☐

Peer ☐

Self ☐

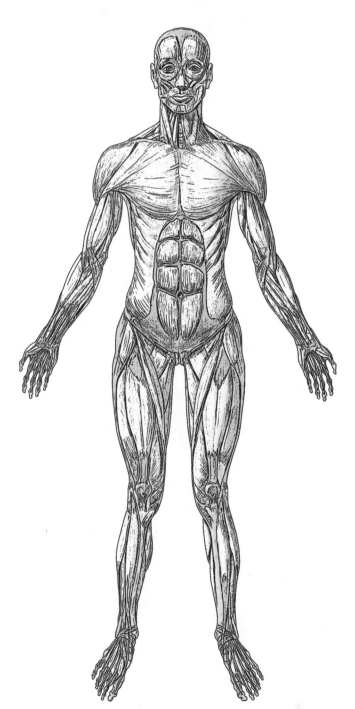

- ☐ Facial Muscles
- ☐ Sternocleido-mastoid
- ☐ Iliopsoas
- ☐ Adductor Longus
- ☐ Deltoids
- ☐ Pectoralis Major
- ☐ Rectus Abdominus
- ☐ Biceps Brachii
- ☐ Brachialis
- ☐ Wrist and Finger Flexors
- ☐ Tensor Fasciae Lata
- ☐ Sartorius
- ☐ Quadriceps Group
- ☐ Tibialis Anterior
- ☐ Tibia

Major Muscles (Posterior)

Mission: Use a different pencil crayon to colour each word on the left-hand side of the page. Then use the same colour to identify the corresponding muscle on the illustration of the posterior muscular system below.

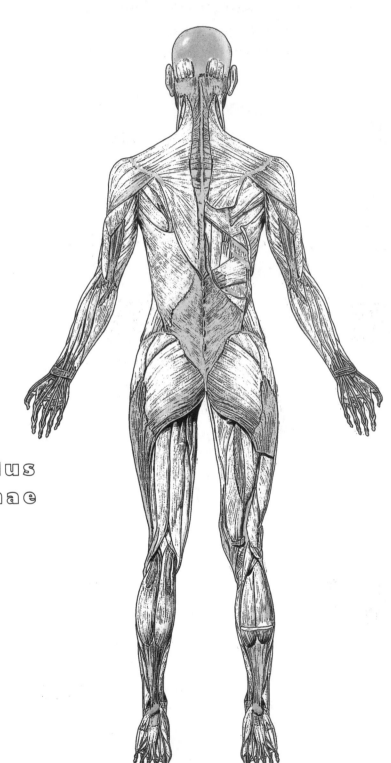

- ☐ Trapezius
- ☐ Latissimus Dorsi
- ☐ Triceps Brachii
- ☐ Gluteus Medius
- ☐ Gluteus Maximus
- ☐ Hamstring Group
- ☐ Gastrocnemius
- ☐ Erector Spinae Group
- ☐ Soleus

Unit 1—Healthy Active Living

Exercise 1.5

Joint Movements

Look in the Book
Pages: 36–37

Understanding the basic movements at your joints gives you a better idea of which exercises you need to focus on to improve your performance in different skills.

Mission: Complete the following diagram by labelling the different joint movements with the terms on the right-hand side of this page.

Student name:

Class/Period:

Date:

Assessed by:

Teacher ☐

Peer ☐

Self ☐

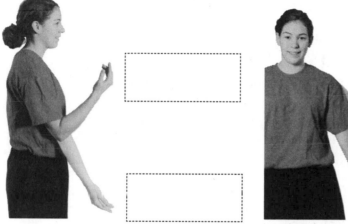

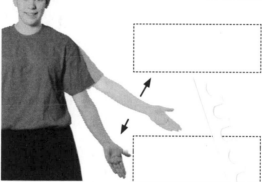

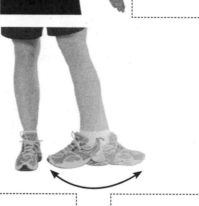

- Eversion
- Inversion
- Flexion
- Extension
- Abduction
- Adduction
- Dorsiflexion
- Plantar flexion
- External rotation
- Internal rotation
- Pronation
- Supination
- Circumduction

Defining Movements at Joints

The following exercise will help you learn the anatomical terms used to describe the movement that occurs at joints.

Mission: Answer the following questions using the terms below.

flexion   extension   abduction   adduction   supination   pronation

dorsiflexion   plantar flexion   inversion   eversion   rotation   circumduction

① What is the movement at the knee joint when your leg moves forward to kick a soccer ball?

② What is the movement at the ankle joint when you're lifting your heels off the ground and keeping your toes and the balls of your feet planted?

③ What is the movement of your ankle joint when you're standing on the inner edge of your foot?

④ What is the movement of your shoulder joint when you raise your arm to the side to stop a goal in soccer?

⑤ What is the movement at your elbow joint when you lift a dumbbell up toward your body?

⑥ What is the rotating action of your hand at the wrist when the palm of your hand is facing upward?

⑦ What is the movement of your ankle joint when you're standing on the outer edge of your foot?

⑧ What movement occurs at your hip joint when you return your leg to the midline of your body while skating?

⑨ What is the movement that occurs when a pitcher throws the ball with a windmill action?

⑩ What is the movement of your ankle joint when you are bringing the top of your foot closer to your shin, which is an essential movement to walking or running?

The Human Heart

Look in the Book
Pages: 42–45

In order to understand how blood flows through the body, you must first become familiar with the main structures of the heart.

Mission: Use a different coloured pencil crayon to colour each word on the right-hand side of the page. Use the same colour to identify the corresponding part on the heart below.

Student name:
Class/Period:
Date:
Assessed by:

Teacher	☐
Peer	☐
Self	☐

☐ Superior and inferior vena cava
☐ Pulmonary arteries
☐ Pulmonary veins
☐ Atria (2)
☐ Ventricles (2)
☐ Aorta
☐ Descending aorta
☐ Pulmonary valve
☐ SA node
☐ AV node
☐ Tricuspid valve
☐ Bicuspid valve
☐ Aortic valve

The Path of Blood

The heart's main function is to pump oxygen-poor (deoxygenated) blood to the lungs, where it is replenished with oxygen, and to pump oxygen-rich (oxygenated) blood out to the body.

Mission: Colour each structure that deoxygenated blood flows through with a blue pencil crayon. Colour each structure that oxygenated blood flows through with a red pencil crayon. Then, with darker coloured red and blue markers, draw arrows to indicate the flow of blood.

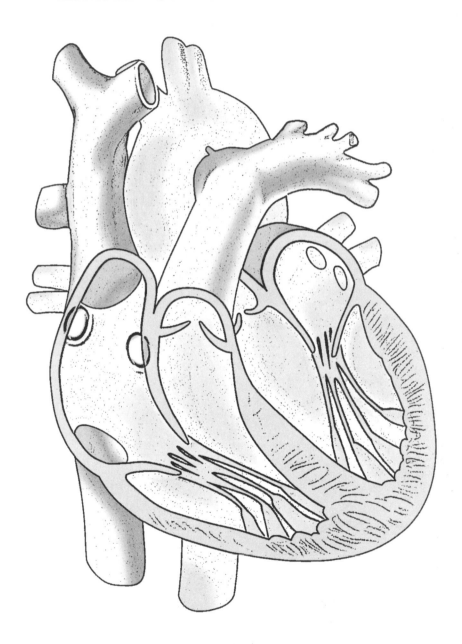

Exercise 1.7

The Respiratory System

The following exercise will help you become familiar with the key components of the respiratory system.

Mission: Use a different coloured pencil crayon to colour each word on the right-hand side of the page. Use the same colour to identify the corresponding part on the diagram below.

☐ Nasal cavity

☐ Trachea

☐ Left lung (2 lobes)

☐ Right lung (3 lobes)

☐ Alveoli

☐ Smooth muscle

☐ Pulmonary arteriole

☐ Pulmonary venule

Keeping Your Cardiorespiratory System Fit

This exercise will help you become familiar with the factors that contribute to keeping the cardiorespiratory system fit.

Mission: The graphic organizer below lists four factors that can affect the health of your cardiorespiratory system. In the space provided for each factor, list some key points about their positive or negative impacts on this important system.

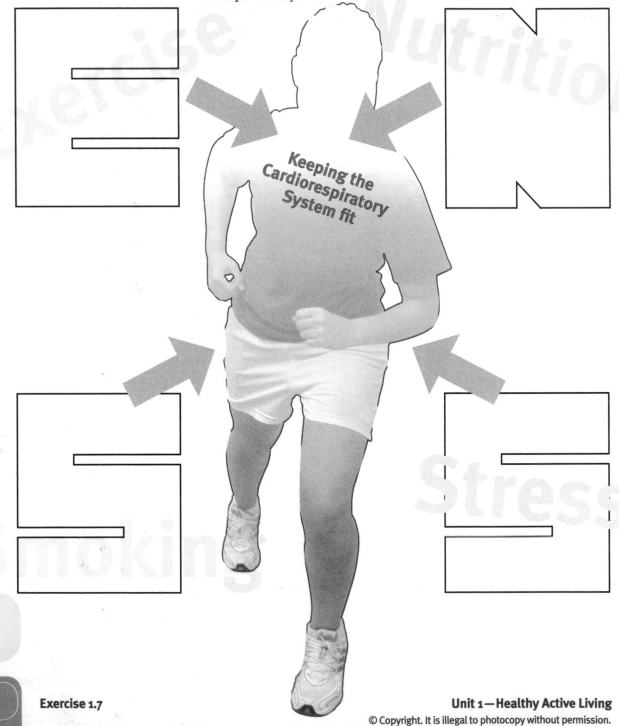

PFP

UNIT 2
Fitness Measurements and Appraisals

What this unit is about ...

➤ Why is it important for me always to stay within my Target Heart Rate Zone when I am involved in various physical activities?

➤ What is musculoskeletal fitness, and why is it important for me to partake in musculoskeletal appraisals?

➤ How can assessing my body composition help me to understand my fitness needs?

KWL for Fitness Appraisals

This exercise will help you and your teacher learn what you know and what you want to know about fitness appraisals. After you have finished, you will be asked to fill out the third column about what you have learned from the experience.

Mission: Complete the "K" column with all the details you **know** about personal fitness appraisals. Record any questions, such as what you **want** to know about personal fitness appraisals, in the "W" column. Choose the fitness appraisals you are going to do, read about them in the textbook, and record any new information that you have **learned** under the "L" column.

KWL FOR PERSONAL FITNESS APPRAISALS

K	W	L
What do I KNOW?	What do I WANT to know?	What have I LEARNED?

Mission: Work with a partner and review your KWL columns together. Fill in any additional details in the "L" column. Then create a graphic organizer, such as a PLACEMAT or a concept map, that brings together all the information listed in the "L" column.

PFP

Exercise 2.1

Finding Your Target Heart Rate Zone

Look in the Book
Pages: 59–61

Follow the four steps below to find your Target Heart Rate Zone. The longer you stay within your zone during a workout, the greater the benefits to your cardiorespiratory system.

Student name: _____

Class/Period: _____

Date: _____

Assessed by: _____

Teacher ☐

Peer ☐

Self ☐

Step 1: Resting Heart Rate

Find your Resting Heart Rate (RHR) by lying down motionless for a couple of minutes. Then take your pulse for 10 seconds and place it into the fomula below:

Heart rate after 10 sec. _____ × 6 = RHR of _____ beats per minute.

Step 2: Maximal Heart Rate

Find your Maximal Heart Rate (MHR) by subtracting your age from 220:

220 bpm – your age = _____ MHR

Step 3: Heart Rate Reserve

Find your Heart Rate Reserve (HRR) by subtracting your RHR from your MHR:

MHR_____ – RHR_____ = _____ HRR

Step 4: Target Heart Rate Zone

Multiply your HRR by .5 (to find the lower limit) or by .85 (to find the upper limit). Then add the result to your RHR to find your Target Heart Rate Zone.

Lower limit of your Target Heart Rate Zone (50%)

HHR _____ × .5 (50%) = _____ + RHR _____ = _____

Upper limit of your Target Heart Rate Zone (85%)

HHR _____ × .85 (85%) = _____ + RHR _____ = _____

After each appraisal period, be sure to recalculate these values, since your heart and its supporting structures will have become stronger— that is, if you worked at it!

PFP

Using a Pedometer

A pedometer is a device that counts how many steps you take over a period of time. Using a pedometer, you can estimate how many kilometres you travelled during a class, a day, or a week. The lab below shows you how to do this.

PART 1: Counting Kilometres

Firmly attach the pedometer to the waistband of your shorts or track pants. To test for the proper placement of the pedometer, follow the steps below:

1. Find an open area where you can take 20 steps without bumping into something or someone. While standing up, open the pedometer and press the reset button until the step count displays the number "0."

2. Close the pedometer and walk normally for 20 steps, counting each step in your head as you go. When you are finished, stop, open the pedometer, and the number "20" should appear in the display. If not, read the manufacturer's instructions again, readjust the pedometer, and follow the steps above until you have proper pedometer placement.

PART 2: Steps per Kilometre

Now that you have your pedometer working properly, find out exactly how many steps you need to take to cover a kilometre (1,000 metres). You will need a track (preferably 400 metres in length) or an open area where 1,000 metres can be covered.

1. Stand on the start line, open your pedometer and press the reset button until the distance count displays the number "0." Begin walking until you have covered a kilometre (1,000 metres, or 2.5 laps using the inside lane of a 400-metre track).

2. After walking a kilometre, open your pedometer and record the value in the blank space below. Most teenagers' values range from 1,100 to 1,400 steps per kilometre.

Step count after 1 km (1,000 m): _____

With this information, you can determine how many kilometres you have covered while participating in H&PE class by using this formula:

$$\text{km covered in class} = \frac{\text{Steps per km}}{\text{Steps in class}}$$

Exercise 2.2

Cardiorespiratory Appraisals

Student name: _____

Class/Period: _____

Date: _____

Assessed by:

Teacher ☐

Peer ☐

Self ☐

A cardiorespiratory fitness appraisal will give you a good indication of your overall fitness. With the help of your teacher, select a cardiorespiratory appraisal that best suits your current level of fitness. If there are medical reasons that you cannot take any of the following appraisals, you should notify your teacher well ahead of time.

mCAFT

Part A: Before You Begin

From the sidebar on page 64 of your Healthy Active Living textbook, find your Starting Stage and Ceiling Heart Rate and record them below.

Starting Stage _____

Ceiling Heart Rate count _____ 10-second count in beats per minute

_____ for heart rate monitor in beats per minute

Part B: Ready Set Go!

If you touch or surpass the Ceiling Heart Rate for your age at any time during the appraisal, you must immediately stop. Record the last stage completed in your activity handbook. Remember, if you have any concerns as to whether you should undertake the mCAFT appraisal, consult with your physical education teacher beforehand.

Record your final heart rate and the final stage you achieved in the space provided below.

Final Heart Rate _____ bpm   Final Stage achieved _____

Part C: Record Your Progress

Record your appraisal date and colour the stage level you achieved in the graph provided.

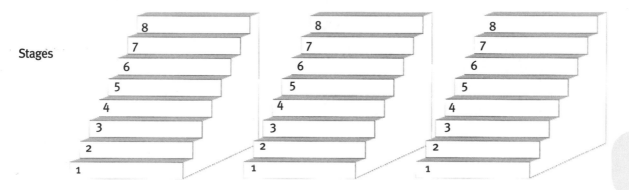

Stages

Date #1 _____   Date #2 _____   Date #3 _____

12-Minute Run

Be sure to perform a good warm up before trying this appraisal. When the appraisal begins, jog or run at a steady pace. Try to keep running throughout, but listen to your body, and stop if your physical condition doesn't allow you to keep running. If you need to walk, do so.

After each appraisal record the number of laps covered in the appropriate lane below. Use the sidebar on the top left-hand corner to convert your laps to kilometres. If you are using a pedometer, record your steps in the sidebar as well.

1 lap = 400 m

½ lap = 200 m

¼ lap = 100 m

1,000 m = 1 km

Pedometer reading

km | steps

Appraisal 1 ____

Appraisal 2 ____

Appraisal 3 ____

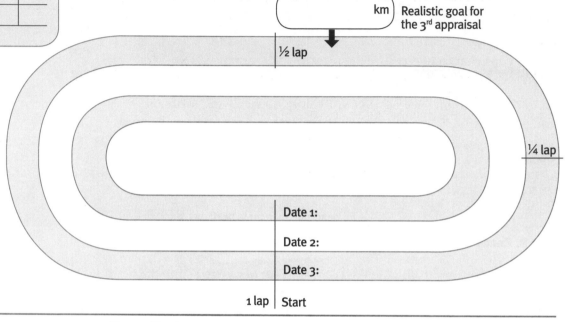

km — Realistic goal for the 3rd appraisal

½ lap

¼ lap

Date 1:

Date 2:

Date 3:

1 lap | Start

Beep Test

The Beep Test is a "maximal" appraisal, which means that at some point you will be going all out. You should attempt this test only if you are in good physical condition and only under the supervision of qualified instructors. If you wish to view your ratings, refer to page 69 in your Healthy Active Living textbook. When you redo this appraisal, your value should increase.

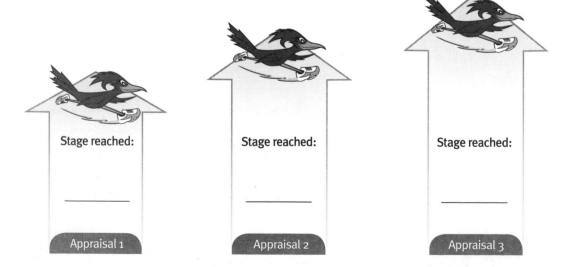

Stage reached: ____ Appraisal 1

Stage reached: ____ Appraisal 2

Stage reached: ____ Appraisal 3

PFP

Exercise 2.3

Muscular Strength and Endurance Appraisals

Look in the Book
Pages: 74–79

These appraisals focus on muscular strength, muscular endurance, and flexibility. You can achieve many health benefits by addressing these aspects of your overall fitness.

Grip Strength

Here is your chance to measure the pressure of your handshake. Write down the results of two separate attempts in the table provided for each appraisal date, then add them together and record your best result in the spaces on the dynamometer below.

1. Date _____ left hand first attempt _____ second attempt _____

   right hand first attempt _____ second attempt _____

2. Date _____ left hand first attempt _____ second attempt _____

   right hand first attempt _____ second attempt _____

3. Date _____ left hand first attempt _____ second attempt _____

   right hand first attempt _____ second attempt _____

Push-Ups

The push-up test measures muscular endurance, specifically that of the deltoids (shoulders), triceps (back of the arm), and the pectoralis major (chest) muscles. Record the dates and write the total number of push-ups you were able to perform in the appropriate areas below.

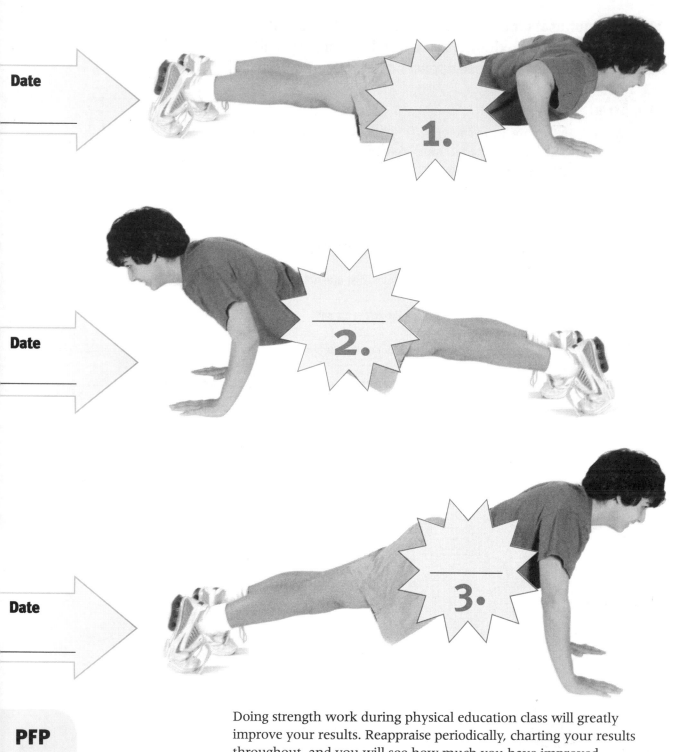

Date
_____

1. _____

Date
_____

2. _____

Date
_____

3. _____

Doing strength work during physical education class will greatly improve your results. Reappraise periodically, charting your results throughout, and you will see how much you have improved.

PFP

Unit 2—Fitness Measurements and Appraisals

Partial Curl-Ups

The abdominal muscles are one of the major muscle groups that make up the "core muscles." This appraisal gives you a good idea of how fit these muscles are. Record the dates and write the total number of partial curl-ups you were able to perform in the appropriate areas below.

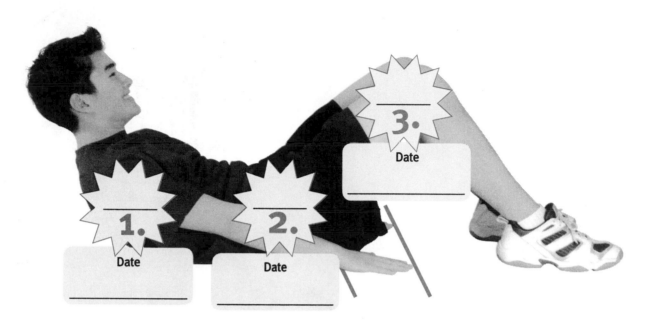

1.
Date

2.
Date

3.
Date

Sit-and-Reach

This appraisal examines the flexibility of your lower back, hamstrings, and calf muscles. Write down the results of two separate attempts in the table provided for each appraisal date, then record your best result in the appropriate areas below.

	First attempt	Second attempt
Date		
Date		
Date		

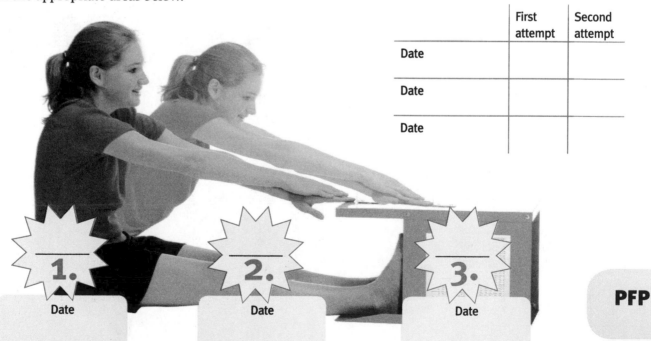

1.
Date

2.
Date

3.
Date

PFP

Unit 2—Fitness Measurements and Appraisals
© Copyright. It is illegal to photocopy without permission.

Exercise 2.3

49

Vertical Jump

The vertical jump appraisal measures how strong your hip and leg muscles are and how much power they can produce. Write down the results of two separate attempts in the arrows provided for each appraisal date, then record your best result in the circles below.

PFP

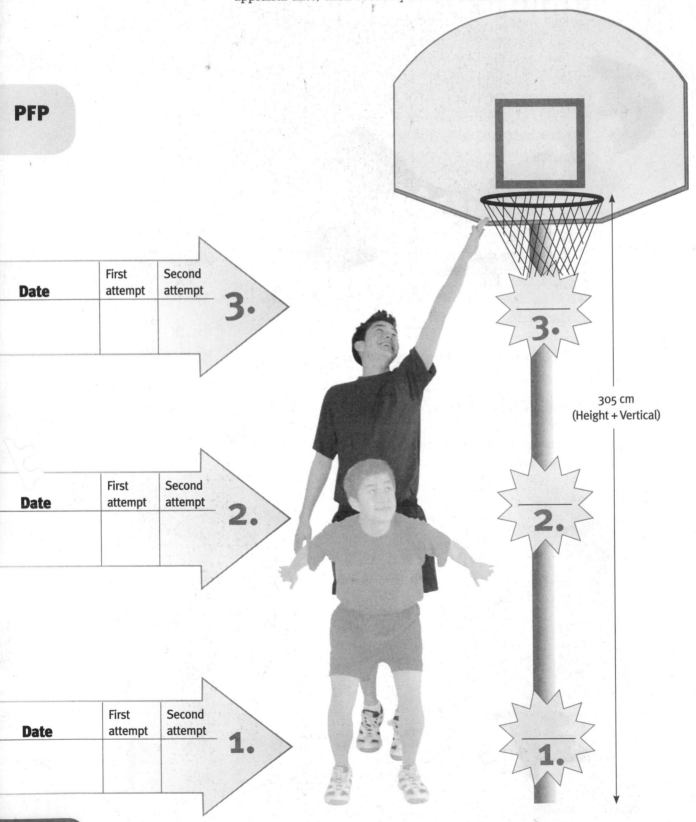

Date	First attempt	Second attempt	**3.**

Date	First attempt	Second attempt	**2.**

Date	First attempt	Second attempt	**1.**

305 cm
(Height + Vertical)

3. _____

2. _____

1. _____

Unit 2—Fitness Measurements and Appraisals

UNIT 3
Fitness Planning, Exercises, and Injury Prevention

What this unit is about ...

➢ Why should I set fitness goals for myself, and how can I make those goals a reality?

➢ Why will knowing and understanding how my major muscles work help me to exercise them in the best way possible?

➢ What does exercise safety mean to me, and why is it important that I follow the appropriate safety measures when involved in various physical activities?

Notes:

Exercise 3.1

My Healthy Active Living Plan

Getting started can be the hardest part of setting goals. The next two exercises will help you focus on exactly what you want to accomplish, and how you can get there.

Student name:

Class/Period:

Date:

Assessed by:

Teacher ☐

Peer ☐

Self ☐

Mission: Complete the Healthy Active Living Plan below using the SMART strategy.

My goal is SPECIFIC because

because I'm scrawny and unhealthy

My goal is MEANINGFUL and MEASURABLE because

My goal is ACTION-ORIENTED because

I will need to weight lift and run not just eat healthy and not junkie

My Healthy Active Living goal is

To gain muscle and run 6 laps without getting dizzie

My goal is REALISTIC because

I haven't set it to high or to small it's something I used to do

My goal is TIME-BOUND because

By the end of the term I can fullfill these goals and maintain them

PFP

My Healthy Active Living Action Plan

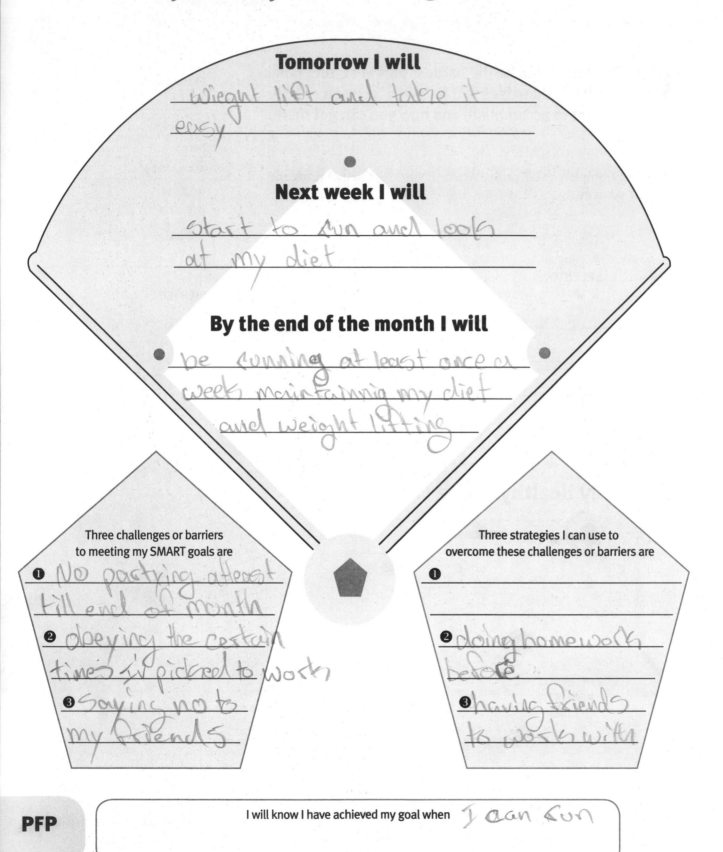

Tomorrow I will

wieght lift and take it easy

Next week I will

start to run and look at my diet

By the end of the month I will

be running at least once a week maintaining my diet and weight lifting

Three challenges or barriers to meeting my SMART goals are

1. No partying atleast till end of month
2. obeying the certain times iv picked to work
3. saying no to my friends

Three strategies I can use to overcome these challenges or barriers are

1.
2. doing homework before
3. having friends to work with

PFP

I will know I have achieved my goal when I can run

Unit 3—Fitness Planning, Exercises, and Injury Prevention

Exercise 3.2

Assessing My Fitness Goals

Look in the Book
Pages: 106–107

When designing a personal fitness program, you need to reappraise your fitness level and reassess your goals on a regular basis. Don't forget to celebrate successes and suggest strategies to overcome any barriers that you experience or may anticipate. The following exercises will help you assess your fitness goals at the beginning, middle, and end of your fitness program.

Student name:

Class/Period:

Date:

Assessed by:

Teacher	☐
Peer	☐
Self	☐

Mission: Complete the following worksheet to help you with this process. Place a checkmark to indicate how far you have progressed on each item.

	THINKING ABOUT IT	BEGINNING	WELL UNDERWAY	DONE!
I created realistic goals for my fitness level.				
I worked on achieving my goals on a regular basis.				
I reassessed my goals and made the appropriate changes.				
I am comfortable in setting fitness goals. I can follow the SMART formula throughout my life.				
I feel that I have achieved a level of fitness that is healthy for me.				

On the continuum below, place an "S" showing where your fitness level was at the start of this term/semester, and place an "N" where you are now.

_____

⓪   ①   ②   ③   ④   ⑤   ⑥   ⑦   ⑧   ⑨   ⑩

What are some things that you would keep the same, or do differently, when creating future fitness goals?

▶ _____   ▶ _____

▶ _____   ▶ _____

▶ _____   ▶ _____

▶ _____   ▶ _____

PFP

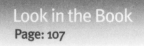

Look in the Book

Page: 107

The FITT Principle

FITT refers to Frequency, Intensity, Time (or duration), and Type of activity. Take all four into account when you plan your fitness program.

Mission: Use this chart to outline your overall fitness program. It will serve as a guide to help you maintain or improve your current fitness level. You can fine-tune it every month.

FITT	CARDIORESPIRATORY	FLEXIBILITY	MUSCULAR ENDURANCE	MUSCULAR STRENGTH
F Frequency				
I Intensity				
T Time				
T Type of activity				

Unit 3—Fitness Planning, Exercises, and Injury Prevention

PFP

Exercise 3.3

Where Do I Go From Here?

Take some time to look back and reflect on what you have achieved this semester. This exercise will help you assess the successes and challenges you may have faced in trying to reach your fitness goals.

Mission: Complete the following worksheet as you reflect on your experience in H&PE class.

Student name:

Class/Period:

Date:

Assessed by:

Teacher ☐

Peer ☐

Self ☐

1. How were you encouraged to achieve your fitness goals?

- _____
- _____
- _____
- _____

2. How were you supported in trying to achieve your fitness goals?

- _____
- _____
- _____
- _____

3. What discouraged you in trying to achieve your fitness goals?

- _____
- _____
- _____
- _____

PFP

4. What did you learn about yourself while trying to reach your fitness goals?

- _____
- _____
- _____
- _____

5. What did you learn about decision making in achieving your fitness goals?

- _____
- _____
- _____
- _____

6. What did you learn that you will use in the future?

- _____
- _____
- _____
- _____

7. What have you learned about fitness and its importance to your daily life?

- _____
- _____
- _____
- _____

PFP

Unit 3—Fitness Planning, Exercises, and Injury Prevention

Resistance Training Log

The weight need not be excessive in order for you to benefit from resistance training. As long as you use moderate weights and closely follow your teacher's directions, you can make resistance training a valuable part of your fitness plan.

Mission: With the help of your Physical Education teacher, fill in the exercises you wish to do during your resistance training unit. Record the starting weight, tempo, and number of repetitions you perform in each set (as instructed by your teacher) in the spaces provided.

EXERCISE	STARTING WEIGHT	TEMPO	SET 1	SET 2	SET 3	REST

PFP

Unit 3—Fitness Planning, Exercises, and Injury Prevention

Resistance Training Log

Exercise	Starting Weight	Tempo	Set 1	Set 2	Set 3	Rest

Period:

Date:

Name:

PFP

UNIT 4
Human Reproduction, Sexuality, and Intimacy

What this unit is about ...

➢ Why is it important for me to take good care of my reproductive system?

➢ What is sexual development, and how do I know if mine is normal?

➢ How can I make good decisions about sexuality and intimacy?

Notes:

Unit 4 — Human Reproduction, Sexuality, and Intimacy

Exercise 4.1

What Do I Know About Human Reproduction, Sexuality, and Intimacy?

The following exercises should be completed without the use of your textbook. Just use your knowledge gained from previous years and apply it to the following questions.

Mission: Using the table below, name the part corresponding to each number on the illustrations of the female and male reproductive systems, and then give a brief description of its function.

#	PART	FUNCTION
❶		
❷		
❸		
❹		
❺		
❻		
❼		
❽		
❾		
❿		

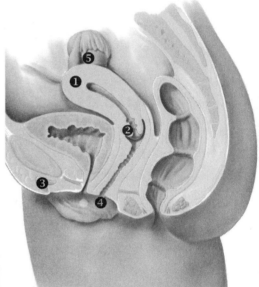

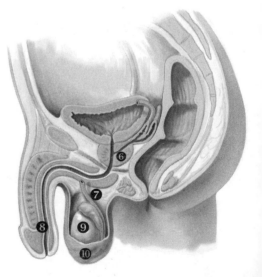

Sexuality: Mix and Match

Mission: Match the terms in column "A" with the most appropriate phrase in column "B." Write your answers in the answer column.

Column A	Answer	Column B
1. Early adulthood		**A.** a person who experiences sexual attraction exclusively towards persons of the same sex
2. Pre-adolescence		**B.** sets of behaviours that project an image of femininity or masculinity
3. Homosexual		**C.** the condition of being female or male as defined by society
4. Sexuality		**D.** a desire to live as a member of the opposite sex but do not undergo Sexual Reassignment Surgery
5. Sex hormones		**E.** a desire to live as a member of the opposite sex resulting in hormonal therapy or Sexual Reassignment Surgery
6. Transsexual		**F.** estrogen in girls and testosterone in boys
7. Transgender		**G.** includes everything that defines us as girls and boys, women and men
8. Gender		**H.** fully developed bodies but still changing emotionally, physically, and socially
9. Gender roles		**I.** between the ages of nine and twelve

Sexuality: Key Terms

Mission: Place the terms below into the sentence that best describes their meaning.

Acquired Immune Deficiency Syndrome   Human Immunodeficiency Virus

condoms   sexually transmitted infections

sexual decision making   abstinence

1. _____ infects the cells in the blood that normally defend against infection.

2. _____ is making conscious choices about your sexual activity.

3. Refraining from sexual intercourse is known as _____.

4. Infections that are transmitted through semen, vaginal fluid, blood, or other body fluids during sexual activity are called _____.

5. _____ occurs when a person's immune system has become so weak that it can no longer successfully fight off infection.

6. Barriers that block bodily fluids from being exchanged during sexual contact are called

_____.

Unit 4—Human Reproduction, Sexuality, and Intimacy

Exercise 4.2

Sexuality: Concept Map

Look in the Book
Page: 169

Sexuality is a term that means different things to different people, so it is important that you have a clear idea of your own opinions and feelings on the subject.

Mission: After reading your Healthy Active Living textbook, reflect on the term sexuality and what it means to you. Brainstorm words associated with or related to sexuality and write them in the spaces provided below.

Student name: _____

Class/Period: _____

Date: _____

Assessed by: _____

Teacher ☐

Peer ☐

Self ☐

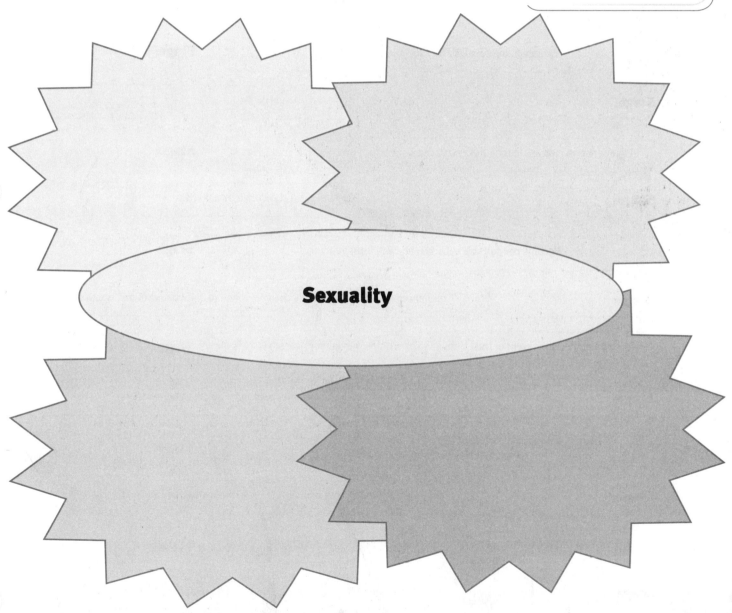

Sexuality

Ages and Stages of Development

Sexuality is always a part of our lives. As we age, we go through various stages of development. These stages are very broad categories, but they can be helpful when trying to understand physical and emotional changes.

Mission: In this exercise, match the stages from the following list to the appropriate stage of sexual development described below.

Stage 1: Infancy (birth–2)

Stage 2: Childhood (3–8)

Stage 3: Pre-adolescence (9–12)

Stage 4: Adolescence (13–18)

Stage 5: Early Adulthood (19–45)

Stage 6: Late Adulthood (46 and up)

Explore body/sexuality through role-playing games **Stage:**

Stage: Begin dating

Experience an increase in their desire for physical intimacy and sexual relationships **Stage:**

Stage: Feel awkward about their own bodies

Become comfortable with sexual identity/orientation **Stage:**

Stage: Experience physical and hormonal changes linked to menopause or andropause

Understand the concept of trust through relationships with parents/caregivers **Stage:**

Stage: Experience an increase in the production of sex hormones

Use words related to sexuality, develop important attitudes about sex from listening to parents/caregivers **Stage:**

Stage: Face pressure to be sexually active whether or not they feel ready

Feel less pressure to behave in gender-specific ways in relationships **Stage:**

Stage: Be increasingly influenced by peers/partners/family/cultural community

Exercise 4.3

Healthy Relationships

Look in the Book
Pages: 188–189

Responsible sexual and intimate decisions are most easily made within healthy relationships. How you feel when you are in a relationship is a sign of whether or not the relationship is healthy for you.

Mission: Before you read your textbook, circle "agree" or "disagree" beside each statement in the table below.

Now read pages 188 and 189 and consider the statements again, based on any new information you may have read, and circle "agree" or "disagree" beside each statement. Look to see whether your opinion has changed.

		Student name:
		Class/Period:
		Date:
		Assessed by:
		Teacher ☐
		Peer ☐
		Self ☐

	BEFORE READING	IN HEALTHY RELATIONSHIPS, PARTNERS...	PAGE #	AFTER READING
1.	Agree Disagree	Disagree and frequently argue over fundamental issues		Agree Disagree
2.	Agree Disagree	Demonstrate trust		Agree Disagree
3.	Agree Disagree	Feel happy and relaxed		Agree Disagree
4.	Agree Disagree	Act with disregard for the other person's feelings		Agree Disagree
5.	Agree Disagree	Have positive self-esteem		Agree Disagree
6.	Agree Disagree	Spend time together and apart		Agree Disagree
7.	Agree Disagree	Feel disrespected and unappreciated		Agree Disagree
8.	Agree Disagree	Enjoy equality		Agree Disagree

BEFORE READING		IN HEALTHY RELATIONSHIPS, PARTNERS...	PAGE #	AFTER READING
9.	Agree Disagree	Do not attempt to understand one another		Agree Disagree
10.	Agree Disagree	Make sexual decisions together		Agree Disagree
11.	Agree Disagree	Are considerate of one another		Agree Disagree
12.	Agree Disagree	Build intimacy through an honest exchange of ideas		Agree Disagree
13.	Agree Disagree	Manipulate one another to get what they want		Agree Disagree
14.	Agree Disagree	Listen to each other		Agree Disagree
15.	Agree Disagree	Do not communicate well		Agree Disagree

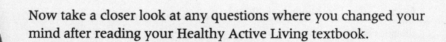

Now take a closer look at any questions where you changed your mind after reading your Healthy Active Living textbook.

What answer surprised you the most?

_____

What did you learn from this exercise?

_____

_____

_____

_____

Unit 4—Human Reproduction, Sexuality, and Intimacy

Exercise 4.4

Sources of Pressure

Sexual decision making entails making conscious choices about sexual activity. Quite often those choices can be influenced by negative factors, such as peer pressure.

Mission: Use the source-effect map below to explore the various sources of pressure to be sexually active. Then list the effects each source of pressure may have on different aspects of a young person's life (e.g., social, emotional, physical).

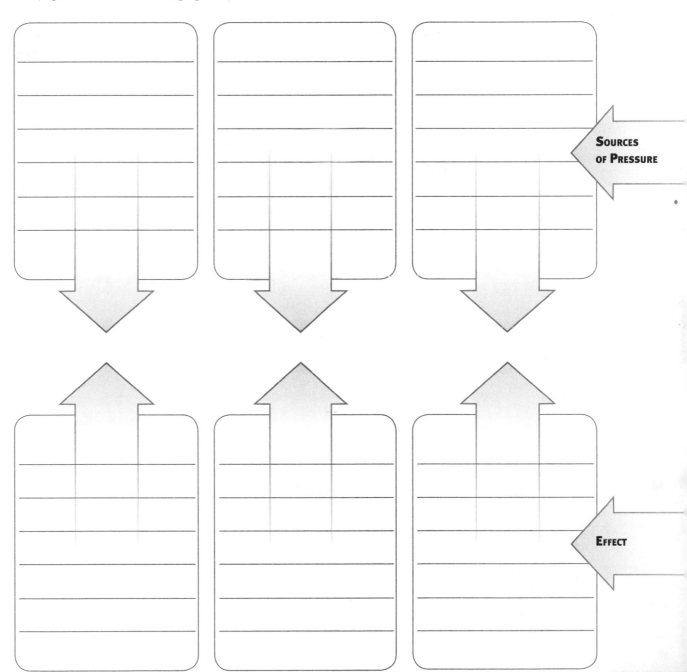

SOURCES OF PRESSURE

EFFECT

He Said/She Said

Since sexuality is so personal, it has a great effect on one's self-esteem. People with a strong sense of self are less likely to compromise their values for the sake of others.

Mission: In this exercise, write down things that you have heard, or that may have been said to you, to sway your decisions regarding sexuality or the pressure to have sex. Then write down what you would say in response.

He/She Said:

The only way our relationship will grow is if we have sex.

You Say:

Our relationship will grow only through trust, mutual respect, and good communication.

He/She Said:

You Say:

He/She Said:

You Say:

He/She Said:

You Say:

He/She Said:

You Say:

Unit 4—Human Reproduction, Sexuality, and Intimacy

Exercise 4.5

Thinking Through Sexual Health Issues

Student name:

Class/Period:

Date:

Assessed by:

Teacher ☐

Peer ☐

Self ☐

This assignment will help you identify and evaluate different approaches to sexual health.

Mission: Choose a health concern associated with sexual activity from the list below or from your reading. On the case file below, identify the nature of the concern, its likely causes, and whom it affects. Research the issue with two different sources (e.g., health professionals, health associations, family or community members), and describe their suggested approaches.

Evaluate the strengths and weaknesses of each approach. For example: Do any of the solutions cause additional health, moral, or ethical concerns? Is one solution more accessible to teens than others?

CONCERNS:

- Teen pregnancy
- HIV/AIDS
- Chlamydia
- Human Papilloma Virus
- Hepatitis B

HEALTH CONCERN: _____

LIKELY CAUSE: _____   **WHOM IT AFFECTS:** _____

SOURCE: _____

SUGGESTED APPROACH: _____

STRENGTHS OF APPROACH: _____   **WEAKNESSES OF APPROACH:** _____

_____   _____

_____   _____

_____   _____

SOURCE: _____

SUGGESTED APPROACH: _____

STRENGTHS OF APPROACH: _____   **WEAKNESSES OF APPROACH:** _____

_____   _____

_____   _____

_____   _____

Unit 4—Human Reproduction, Sexuality, and Intimacy

Exercise 4.5

Community Services

Mission: Using the table below, identify services available in your community for people needing advice on, or help with, sexual decision making, contraception, or other matters related to sexuality.

1.

NAME OF SUPPORT SERVICE	SERVICES PROVIDED TO COMMUNITY	PROFESSIONAL PERSONNEL ON STAFF	CONTACT INFORMATION

2.

NAME OF SUPPORT SERVICE	SERVICES PROVIDED TO COMMUNITY	PROFESSIONAL PERSONNEL ON STAFF	CONTACT INFORMATION

3.

NAME OF SUPPORT SERVICE	SERVICES PROVIDED TO COMMUNITY	PROFESSIONAL PERSONNEL ON STAFF	CONTACT INFORMATION

Unit 4—Human Reproduction, Sexuality, and Intimacy

UNIT 5
Drug Use and Abuse

What this unit is about ...

➢ Why do some people use harmful drugs and what are the possible health consequences?

➢ What are the short- and long-term health effects of tobacco and alcohol on the body?

➢ What are the illegal drugs and what options are available for those who have become dependent on them?

Notes:

Exercise 5.1

What Do I Know About Drugs?

The following exercises should be completed without the use of your textbook. Just use your knowledge gained from previous years and apply it to the following questions.

Student name:

Class/Period:

Date:

Assessed by:

Teacher ☐

Peer ☐

Self ☐

Mission: Read each statement and decide whether you think they are "True" or "False."

① Drugs are any substance that affects a person's mental, emotional, or physical state.	TRUE ☐	FALSE ☐
Rationale:			

② Hallucinogens can affect vision, hearing, smell, and touch.	TRUE ☐	FALSE ☐
Rationale:			

③ Cannabis (Marijuana) acts as a hallucinogen and as a stimulant, but it does not act as a depressant.	TRUE ☐	FALSE ☐
Rationale:			

④ Nicotine, caffeine, and cocaine are all various forms of stimulants.	TRUE ☐	FALSE ☐
Rationale:			

⑤ Anabolic steroids, when used to enhance athletic performance and body image, cause no physical or psychological side effects.	TRUE ☐	FALSE ☐
Rationale:			

⑥ Depressants slow down various body systems and reduce inhibitions.	TRUE ☐	FALSE ☐
Rationale:			

⑦ Magic mushrooms, LSD, and mescaline are all forms of depressants.	TRUE ☐	FALSE ☐
Rationale:			

Tobacco and Alcohol: Mix and Match

Mission: Match the terms in column A with the appropriate phrase in column B. Write your answers in the answer column provided for you.

COLUMN A	ANSWER	COLUMN B
1. Nicotine		**A.** Amount of alcohol in a person's bloodstream
2. Tar		**B.** Control the sale and advertising of alcohol
3. 0.08 grams		**C.** Produced by fermenting or distilling various fruits, vegetables, or grains
4. Tobacco		**D.** Using alcohol in a way that causes problems for the individual or for others around that person
5. Snuff		**E.** An addiction to alcohol
6. Alcohol		**F.** National legal limit for impaired driving per 100 ml of blood
7. Blood-Alcohol content		**G.** One of the most addictive substances known to scientists
8. Alcohol Abuse		**H.** Dried leaves which can be smoked or chewed
9. Liquor Control regulations		**I.** A cancer-causing chemical found in tobacco smoke
10. Alcohol Dependence		**J.** Smokeless tobacco

Marijuana, Illegal Drugs, and Steroids

Mission: Place the terms below into the sentence that best describes their meaning.

date-rape   inhalants   performance-enhancing   acid
crack   cannabis

1. _____ is the plant from which marijuana is produced.

2. Lysergic acid diethylamide, a hallucinogen, is commonly known as _____.

3. _____ is a smokeable, freebase form of cocaine.

4. GHB, ketamine, and Rohypnol are the drugs that are often referred to as

_____ drugs.

5. _____ produce a feeling of euphoria and light-headedness while slowing down body systems.

6. Anabolic steroids are classified as _____ drugs.

Exercise 5.2

Drugs and Their Effects

Look in the Book
Page: 247

Drugs are substances that affect a person's mental, emotional, or physical state. There are five main classifications of drugs: stimulants, depressants, hallucinogens, cannabis, and anabolic steroids.

Mission: Use the space provided in the table below to briefly identify each type of drug by providing examples, listing the drug's common (or street) names, and recording the mental, emotional, or physical effects these drugs have on a person.

Student name:

Class/Period:

Date:

Assessed by:

Teacher ☐

Peer ☐

Self ☐

CLASSIFICATION	EXAMPLES	COMMON NAMES (STREET NAMES)	EFFECTS
STIMULANTS			
DEPRESSANTS			
HALLUCINOGENS			
CANNABIS			
ANABOLIC STEROIDS			

Continuum of Risk

Using drugs for non-medical reasons almost always poses some degree of risk. The continuum of risk is a way of measuring drug use and the risks associated with it.

Mission: Identify the level of risk of drug use that each student is experiencing in the following scenarios.

❶ Johnny is using marijuana frequently. He cuts class and neglects his school work so that he can hang out with his friends who also use marijuana. His grades are declining, his mood has become anxious, and sometimes he has trouble concentrating.

Level of risk: - ➤

What advice would you give Johnny?

❷ Gina's friends are cigarette smokers. They have teased Gina for not smoking and have encouraged her to try. Scared that she might lose her friends or appear "un-cool," Gina has tried smoking just a couple of times.

Level of risk: - ➤

What advice would you give Gina?

❸ Aaron uses cocaine because of the immediate effects of the drug. He doesn't use it often, but now he needs to use more cocaine to get that "high" he enjoys so much.

Level of risk: - ➤

What advice would you give Aaron?

❹ Maggie is in the chess club, the student council, and she is the captain of the girls' indoor field hockey team. She refuses to try smoking, drinking, or any other form of substance because she wants to enjoy a healthy, active lifestyle.

Level of risk: - ➤

What advice would you give Maggie?

Myths and Facts about Drug Use

Illegal drugs have become increasingly available in Canada. Young people need good information in order to make health-conscious decisions about substances.

Student name:

Class/Period:

Date:

Assessed by:

Teacher ☐

Peer ☐

Self ☐

Mission: Before you read your textbook, circle "agree" or "disagree" beside each statement in the table below. Now read Chapter 13 and consider the statements again, based on any new information you may have read. Again, circle "agree" or "disagree" beside each statement. Look to see whether your opinion has changed.

	BEFORE READING	STATEMENTS	PAGE #	AFTER READING
1.	Agree Disagree	Internet, TV, and movies can often influence teens to try various substances.		Agree Disagree
2.	Agree Disagree	Teens are curious by nature and want to experiment with drugs to see what the effects are like.		Agree Disagree
3.	Agree Disagree	The desire to be accepted may result in teens trying substances to avoid being teased or left out.		Agree Disagree
4.	Agree Disagree	Being well informed of the risks associated with drug use helps teens to avoid using them.		Agree Disagree
5.	Agree Disagree	Rebelling and the desire to make their own decisions is often a reason that teens try/use drugs.		Agree Disagree
6.	Agree Disagree	Teens experiencing emotional stress may use drugs as a "quick fix" to their problems.		Agree Disagree
7.	Agree Disagree	Teens use drugs to help them feel confident.		Agree Disagre
8.	Agree Disagree	Teens often try various substances to help them stay awake and gain an edge.		Agree Disagree
9.	Agree Disagree	Teens try drugs to help them lose weight or gain muscle mass.		Agree Disagree

BEFORE READING	STATEMENTS	PAGE #	AFTER READING
10. Agree Disagree	Teens often think that using various substances will help them focus and concentrate better.		Agree Disagree
11. Agree Disagree	Teens suffering from clinical mental health problems risk substance abuse when they try various drugs to "self-medicate" their distress .		Agree Disagree
12. Agree Disagree	Alcohol is often valued as a symbolic importance when used in religious services or family/community celebrations.		Agree Disagree
13. Agree Disagree	Loneliness is one reason that teens try various substances.		Agree Disagree
14. Agree Disagree	Teenagers are more likely than adults to drink or use drugs past the point of intoxication.		Agree Disagree
15. Agree Disagree	If a person is using a substance in order to "cope" with other problems, such as stress, shyness, or pain, that person is abusing the substance.		Agree Disagree
16. Agree Disagree	Being physically active and playing sports is extremely dangerous if someone is taking drugs of any kind.		Agree Disagree
17. Agree Disagree	A person who has an overwhelming desire to repeat the effects of a drug is in serious need of help and professional counselling.		Agree Disagree

Now take a closer look at any statements where you changed your mind after reading your Healthy Active Living textbook.

What answer surprised you the most?

_____

What did you learn from this exercise?

_____

_____

_____

Unit 5—Drug Use and Abuse

Exercise 5.4

Tobacco and Alcohol

Look in the Book
Pages: 231 & 237

Tobacco and alcohol are the only controlled mood-altering substances permitted for non-medical use in Canada. However, they both pose serious short- and long-term health effects.

Mission: Describe the health effects of tobacco or alcohol on the body by using arrows to point to the body parts affected and listing how they are affected.

Student name: _____

Class/Period: _____

Date: _____

Assessed by:

Teacher ☐

Peer ☐

Self ☐

Media Analysis

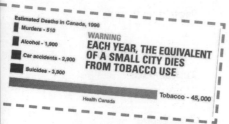

Estimated Deaths in Canada, 1996
Murders - 510
Alcohol - 1,900
Car accidents - 2,900
Suicides - 3,900
Tobacco - 45,000
Health Canada

WARNING
EACH YEAR, THE EQUIVALENT OF A SMALL CITY DIES FROM TOBACCO USE

Mission: Take two different cigarette ads or alcohol ads from a magazine or the Internet—one promoting the product and one deterring interest in the product. Try to find similar media tactics within the ads. Also look at the presentation of the ads—the colours, graphics, content of text, and images portrayed. Write the comparisons in the table below.

COMPARISONS	PROMOTIONAL AD	DETERRENT AD
Similarities		
Differences		

Exercise 5.5

Marijuana and Other Illegal Drugs

Look in the Book
Page: 246

The "Gateway Theory" of drug use proposes that someone who uses marijuana is more likely than a non-user to go on to use more serious drugs.

Mission: Review the evidence that supports/opposes the Gateway Theory of drug use and decide whether you agree or disagree with this theory. Give examples that might support your viewpoint. Share your arguments with your classmates and add some of their points to your version of the table.

Student name:

Class/Period:

Date:

Assessed by:

Teacher ☐

Peer ☐

Self ☐

SUPPORTS	BOTH SIDES NOW	OPPOSES
	Is Marijuana a Gateway drug?	

Decision Making—IDEAL in Action

Mission: Create a scenario involving a decision about drugs and identify the basic problem. Outline options for dealing with the situation, and evaluate the pros and cons of each choice. Use the IDEAL model below to arrive at a decision. Explain why you made that decision and what you learned from the experience.

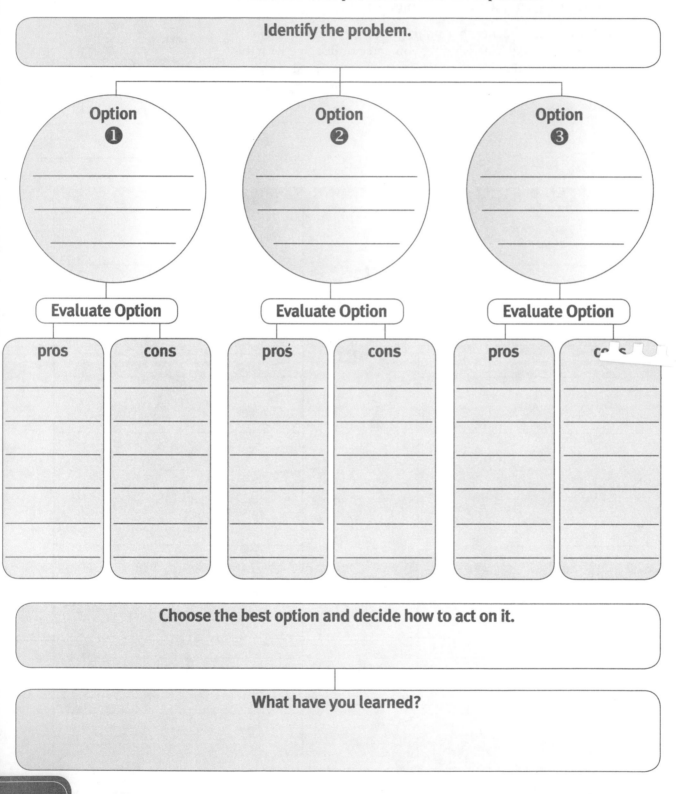

Identify the problem.

Option ❶

_____

_____

_____

Option ❷

_____

_____

_____

Option ❸

_____

_____

_____

Evaluate Option

pros	cons

Evaluate Option

pros	cons

Evaluate Option

pros	cons

Choose the best option and decide how to act on it.

What have you learned?

Exercise 5.6

Drug Use and Abuse—Key Terms

You should now have a greater understanding of substance use and abuse, and the detrimental effects they have on your physical and psychological well-being.

Mission: Briefly explain the meaning of the following key terms.

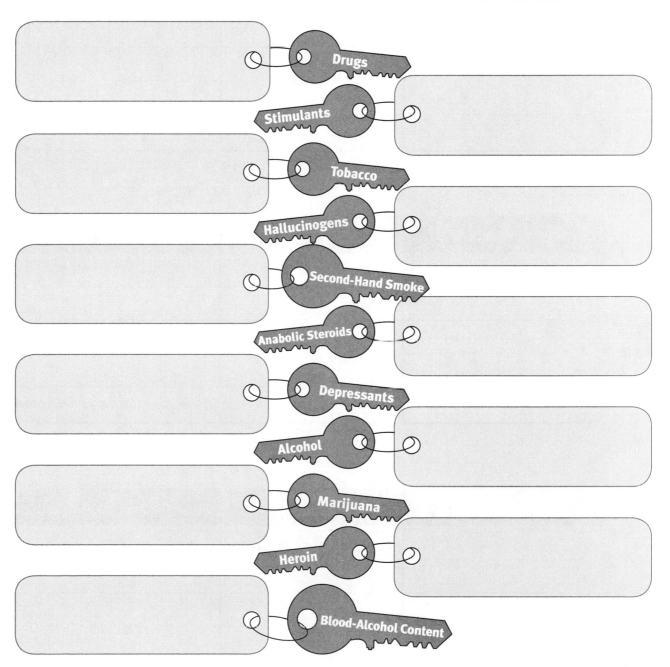

School and Community Strategies to Combat Drug Abuse

Mission: List three websites, other than the ones indicated in your textbook, that provide information on smoking, alcohol abuse, and drug abuse.

1.

WEBSITE	SERVICES/INFO AVAILABLE	CONTACT INFO AVAILABLE ON WEBSITE

2.

WEBSITE	SERVICES/INFO AVAILABLE	CONTACT INFO AVAILABLE ON WEBSITE

3.

WEBSITE	SERVICES/INFO AVAILABLE	CONTACT INFO AVAILABLE ON WEBSITE

UNIT 6
Conflict Resolution and Personal Safety

What this unit is about ...

➤ Why will understanding conflict help me to deal with conflict?

➤ What forms of violence have I witnessed in the past, and what can I do to ensure that I don't become a victim or a perpetrator of violence?

Notes:

Exercise 6.1

What Do I Know About Violence and Conflict?

The following exercise should be completed without the use of your textbook. Just use your knowledge gained from previous years and apply it to the following questions.

Mission: Read each statement and decide whether you think they are "True" or "False."

Student name:
_____

Class/Period: _____
Date: _____
Assessed by: _____
Teacher ☐
Peer ☐
Self ☐

❶ A certain amount of conflict is a natural and essential part of learning and growing.	TRUE ☐	FALSE ☐

Rationale:

❷ Internal conflicts are the conflicting emotions you feel within yourself.	TRUE ☐	FALSE ☐

Rationale:

❸ Intra-group conflicts are conflicts that occur when two groups or teams come together in opposition.	TRUE ☐	FALSE ☐

Rationale:

❹ Conflict resolution or coping skills are ways to deal with, manage, or accept stressful situations.	TRUE ☐	FALSE ☐

Rationale:

❺ A person who has good perceptive abilities is unable to see a situation from the other person's perspective.	TRUE ☐	FALSE ☐

Rationale:

❻ If you remain assertive in a conflict, it does not mean that you are being aggressive or bullying.	TRUE ☐	FALSE ☐

Rationale:

❼ Behind most anger is fear.	TRUE ☐	FALSE ☐

Rationale:

Combatting Violence, Creating Safe Schools

Mission: Place the terms below into the sentence that best describe their meaning.

bullying   violence   indirect bullying   M for Mature

sexual harassment   dating violence   racism

cyber-bullying   hate crime   Charter of Rights and Freedoms

1. _____ is the intentional use of aggression to injure or intimidate someone.

2. It is illegal to sell or rent video games marked _____ to anyone under 17 years of age in Nova Scotia, Ontario, and Manitoba.

3. Intimidation, aggression, and acts of violent behaviour towards someone are all tactics used for

_____.

4. _____ is bullying that occurs via the use of websites, emails, and phone or text messages.

5. _____ includes taunts, threats, intimidation, extortion, and exclusion. It is very difficult to detect and is becoming increasingly common among males.

6. _____ is defined as one racial group believing they are superior to another, and the prejudicial or violent behaviours shown toward other races as a result of this attitude.

7. The _____ is a document adopted by the Canadian government to ensure equality and protect the rights of all Canadians in every province and territory.

8. Any sexual, physical, or psychological attack on one partner by the other in a dating relationship is

called _____.

9. A _____ is a crime committed against a person or group of people who can be distinguished by colour, race, religion, ethnic origin, or sexual orientation.

10. Making sexual comments or pressuring someone to have sex is usually called

_____.

Exercise 6.2

Types of Conflict

Look in the Book
Pages: 264–265

There are many different types of conflict and many different reasons why they arise. The best way to avoid conflict is to learn what causes a person to become angry and how best to avoid these situations.

Student name:

Class/Period:

Date:

Assessed by:

Teacher ☐

Peer ☐

Self ☐

Mission: Before learning to resolve conflict you must understand what type of conflict you are dealing with. Use the worksheet below to help you gain an understanding of the various types of conflict and ways of dealing with each one.

TYPE OF CONFLICT	DEFINITION	EXAMPLE	WAY OF DEALING WITH IT
INTERNAL CONFLICT			
INTERPERSONAL CONFLICT			
INTRA-GROUP CONFLICT			
INTER-GROUP CONFLICT			

Triggers of Anger and Anger Management

Mission: Complete the sentence stems below to identify the situations that make you angry, and different ways of dealing with it.

Things that make me angry are _____

_____

_____

I usually get angry because_____

_____

_____

_____

When I am angry, I _____

_____

_____

To calm myself down when I am angry, I _____

_____

_____

The people that I tend to get angry at the most are_____

_____

_____

List four things that help you cope with and reduce the onset of your anger:

1._____

_____

2. _____

_____

3. _____

_____

4. _____

_____

Types of Abuse and Violence

Look in the Book
Pages: 274–287

Abuse can take many forms, such as physical, sexual, or psychological abuse; sexual- or gender-based harassment; racial harassment; hate crimes; bullying; and gang violence. These exercises will help you become familiar with the different types of violence and abuse, and the effects these can have on the victims.

Mission: In the table below, define each type of abuse in the space provided.

Student name: _____

Class/Period: _____

Date: _____

Assessed by:

Teacher ☐

Peer ☐

Self ☐

TYPE OF ABUSE	DEFINITIONS
VIOLENCE	
PHYSICAL ABUSE	
PSYCHOLOGICAL ABUSE	
GANG VIOLENCE	
BULLYING	
DATING VIOLENCE	
SEXUAL HARASSMENT	
HATE CRIMES	
RACISM	
HOMOPHOBIC VIOLENCE	

Impact of Non-Physical Abuse

Mission: Answer the following questions in the spaces provided.

1. Explain what cyber-bullying is and the effects it can have on the victim.

_____

_____

_____

_____

2. Demonstrate why verbal or indirect bullying is considered a form of psychological abuse. Give some examples, and describe how this method of abuse affects the victim.

_____

_____

_____

_____

3. Canada is a multicultural society, yet hate crimes and racism are still prevalent in schools. What are some of the emotional challenges victims of hate crimes and racism must endure?

_____

_____

_____

_____

4. Explain why you do—or do not—believe that verbal or indirect bullying can leave lifelong emotional scars on the victims.

_____

_____

_____

_____

5. What are some of the recognizable signs of psychological abuse? List some of the measures one can take to get out of an abusive situation.

_____

_____

_____

Unit 6—Conflict Resolution and Personal Safety

Exercise 6.4

Effects of Abuse and Violence

The following exercises will help you learn more about the causes of abuse and violence, and the effects they can have on victims.

Mission: Choose one of the case studies below, and answer the questions in the space provided.

Student name: _____

Class/Period: _____

Date: _____

Assessed by: _____

Teacher ☐

Peer ☐

Self ☐

Case Study #1:

Jake is playing soccer one afternoon in H&PE class. He is dribbling down the field with the ball when someone on the opposing team sticks a foot out and trips him. Jake lies on the ground, waiting for the teacher to call a foul, but nothing happens. The other player takes the ball and and scores on Jake's team. Jake jumps up and chases after the person who tripped him. He shoves the other player and yells at him. A fight breaks out.

Case Study #2:

Christine takes a math class with a group of girls that she doesn't know very well, but who are always giving her a hard time. They laugh at her behind her back and make fun of her anytime she speaks in class. So far she has ignored them, but lately their behaviour has grown worse. Last week she found out that they were making up stories about her and telling them to other people, and this week she received three rude emails that made her very uncomfortable. She feels anxious every time she has to go to math class and thinks about skipping so she can avoid seeing the girls entirely.

1. What kind of violence/abuse is depicted here?

2. How do you think the victim is feeling in this situation?

3. What do you think was the cause of the problem?

4. What impact will this situation have on the victim?

5. How did the story make you feel?

6. What do you think the victim's options are in this situation?

PLACEMAT: Solutions and Strategies

Mission: What words, ideas, or experiences come to mind when you hear the word "abuse"? Which ones have you witnessed or experienced at school, in your community, or in the media? Write down your thoughts on one of the four corner squares. Ask three different classmates to each fill in a different corner. Then, as a group of four, circle ideas you all had in common, and write one or two sentences that sum up the meaning of "Abuse" in the middle square.

ABUSE

Exercise 6.5

Conflict Resolution and Personal Safety—Key Terms

Look in the Book
Pages: 274–287

You should now have a greater understanding of different types of abuse and violence that exist, the impact on victims, and some of their causes.

Mission: Briefly explain the meaning of the following key terms.

Student name:

Class/Period:

Date:

Assessed by:

Teacher ☐

Peer ☐

Self ☐

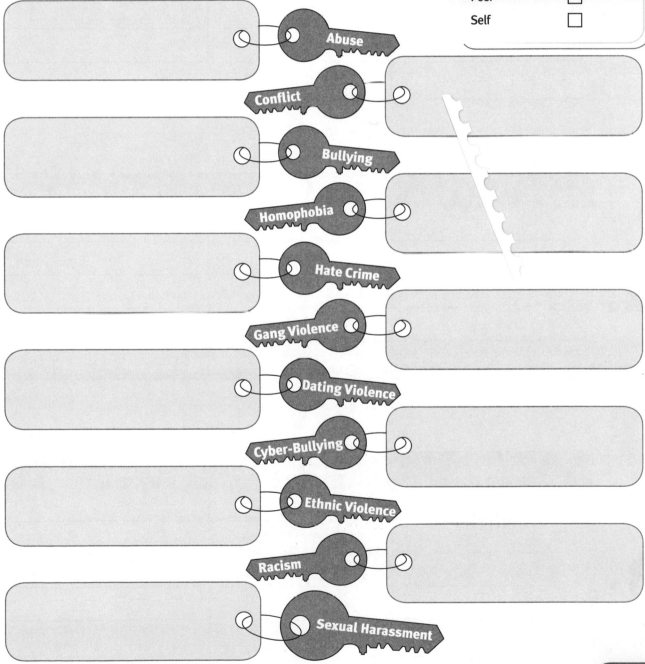

Abuse

Conflict

Bullying

Homophobia

Hate Crime

Gang Violence

Dating Violence

Cyber-Bullying

Ethnic Violence

Racism

Sexual Harassment

Building Safe Communities

Mission: List three websites, other than the ones listed in your textbook, that provide information and support on abuse, violence, and victims of abuse.

1.

WEBSITE	SERVICES/INFO AVAILABLE	CONTACT INFO AVAILABLE ON WEBSITE

2.

WEBSITE	SERVICES/INFO AVAILABLE	CONTACT INFO AVAILABLE ON WEBSITE

3.

WEBSITE	SERVICES/INFO AVAILABLE	CONTACT INFO AVAILABLE ON WEBSITE

Unit 6—Conflict Resolution and Personal Safety

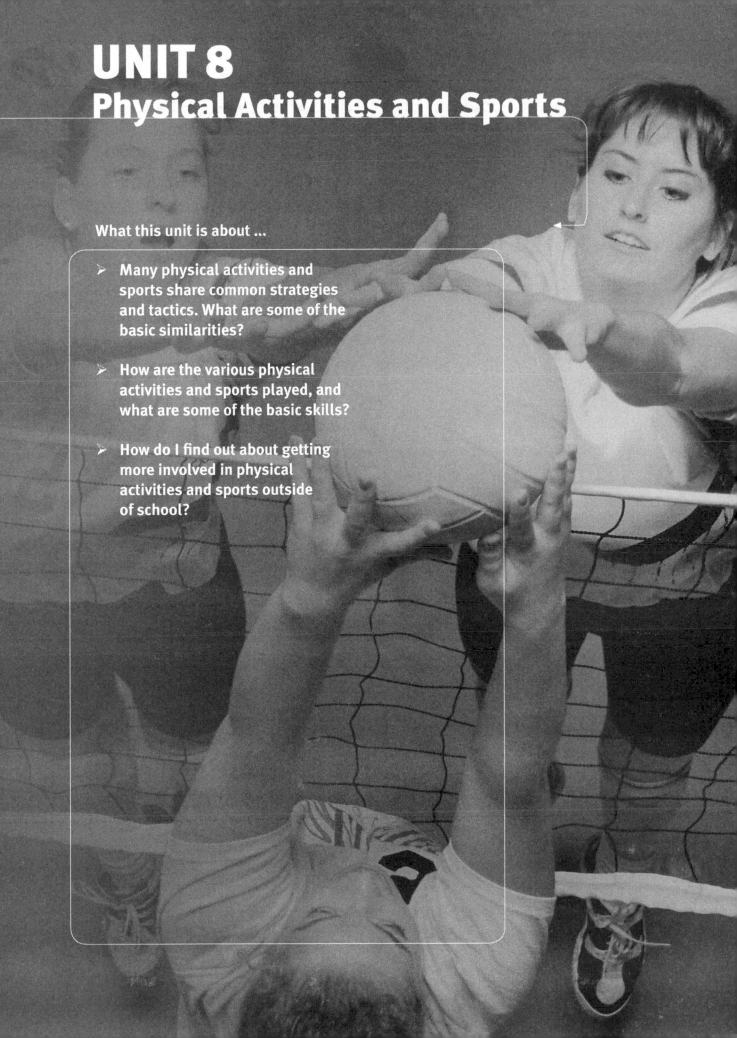

UNIT 8
Physical Activities and Sports

What this unit is about ...

➢ Many physical activities and sports share common strategies and tactics. What are some of the basic similarities?

➢ How are the various physical activities and sports played, and what are some of the basic skills?

➢ How do I find out about getting more involved in physical activities and sports outside of school?

Notes:

Unit 8 — Physical Activites and Sports

Exercise 8.1

Invasion/Territory Games

Invasion/territory games are some of the most common games that we play. They include sports such as soccer, basketball, ultimate, ice hockey, field hockey, rugby, football, and lacrosse, just to mention a few.

Look in the Book
Page: 337

Student name:

Class/Period:

Date:

Assessed by:

Teacher ☐

Peer ☐

Self ☐

Strategies and Tactics

Mission: Complete the chart below outlining the general strategies and tactics that are used in invasion/territory games. For each strategy and tactical situation, provide sport-specific examples.

STRATEGIES AND TACTICS ON OFFENCE	**STRATEGIES AND TACTICS ON DEFENCE**
Overall strategy:	Overall strategy:
Sport-specific strategy:	Sport-specific strategy:

Phases of a Skill

Mission: Choose a skill from one of the invasion/territory games covered in this chapter. Identify some key points involved in the preparation, execution, and follow-through of this skill and record them on the chart below. Use the "Yes" and "No" columns for self-evaluation, or evaluation by a peer or teacher.

SPORT	NAME		
	SKILL	**YES**	**NO**
Preparation		☐	☐
		☐	☐
		☐	☐
		☐	☐
		☐	☐
		☐	☐
		☐	☐
		☐	☐
Execution		☐	☐
		☐	☐
		☐	☐
		☐	☐
		☐	☐
		☐	☐
		☐	☐
		☐	☐
Follow-Through		☐	☐
		☐	☐
		☐	☐
		☐	☐
		☐	☐
		☐	☐
		☐	☐
		☐	☐

Exercise 8.2

Net/Wall Games

Look in the Book
Page: 371

Net/wall games are popular sports that many Canadians enjoy playing. They include sports such as volleyball, badminton, tennis, table tennis, squash, racquetball, and handball.

Student name:

_____

Class/Period:

Date:

Assessed by:

Teacher ☐

Peer ☐

Self ☐

Strategies and Tactics

Mission: Complete the chart below outlining the general strategies and tactics that are used in net/wall games. For each strategy and tactical situation, provide sport-specific examples.

STRATEGIES AND TACTICS ON OFFENCE	STRATEGIES AND TACTICS ON DEFENCE
Overall strategy:	Overall strategy:
Sport-specific strategy:	Sport-specific strategy:

Phases of a Skill

Mission: Choose a skill from one of the net/wall games covered in this chapter. Identify some key points involved in the preparation, execution, and follow-through of this skill and record them on the chart below. Use the "Yes" and "No" columns for self-evaluation, or evaluation by a peer or teacher.

SPORT	NAME		
	SKILL	YES	NO
Preparation		☐	☐
		☐	☐
		☐	☐
		☐	☐
		☐	☐
		☐	☐
		☐	☐
		☐	☐
Execution		☐	☐
		☐	☐
		☐	☐
		☐	☐
		☐	☐
		☐	☐
		☐	☐
		☐	☐
Follow-Through		☐	☐
		☐	☐
		☐	☐
		☐	☐
		☐	☐
		☐	☐
		☐	☐
		☐	☐

Striking/Fielding Games

Look in the Book
Page: 389

In striking/fielding games, such as baseball, softball, and cricket, a player on the defensive team delivers the ball to a player on the offensive team. The batter attempts to strike the ball and score by running between safe areas without the ball being caught, or by reaching the safe area.

Strategies and Tactics

Mission: Complete the chart below outlining the general strategies and tactics that arc uscd in striking/ficlding gamcs. For cach stratcgy and tactical situation, provide sport-specific examples.

Student name:	
Class/Period:	
Date:	
Assessed by:	
Teacher	☐
Peer	☐
Self	☐

STRATEGIES AND TACTICS ON OFFENCE	STRATEGIES AND TACTICS ON DEFENCE
Overall strategy:	Overall strategy:
Sport-specific strategy:	Sport-specific strategy:

Phases of a Skill

Mission: Choose a skill from one of the striking/fielding games covered in this chapter. Identify some key points involved in the preparation, execution, and follow-through of this skill and record them on the chart below. Use the "Yes" and "No" columns for self-evaluation, or evaluation by a peer or teacher.

SPORT	NAME		
	SKILL	YES	NO
Preparation		☐	☐
		☐	☐
		☐	☐
		☐	☐
		☐	☐
		☐	☐
		☐	☐
		☐	☐
Execution		☐	☐
		☐	☐
		☐	☐
		☐	☐
		☐	☐
		☐	☐
		☐	☐
		☐	☐
Follow-Through		☐	☐
		☐	☐
		☐	☐
		☐	☐
		☐	☐
		☐	☐
		☐	☐
		☐	☐

Exercise 8.4

Target Games

Look in the Book
Page: 399

Student name:

Class/Period:

Date:

Assessed by:

Teacher ☐

Peer ☐

Self ☐

The two target games discussed in this unit—curling and golf—are among the most popular sporting activities. Other target games include bowling, archery, billiards, bocce, croquet, darts, horseshoe pitching, shuffleboard, and lawn bowling.

Strategies and Tactics

Mission: Complete the chart below outlining the general strategies and tactics that are used in target games. For each strategy and tactical situation, provide sport-specific examples.

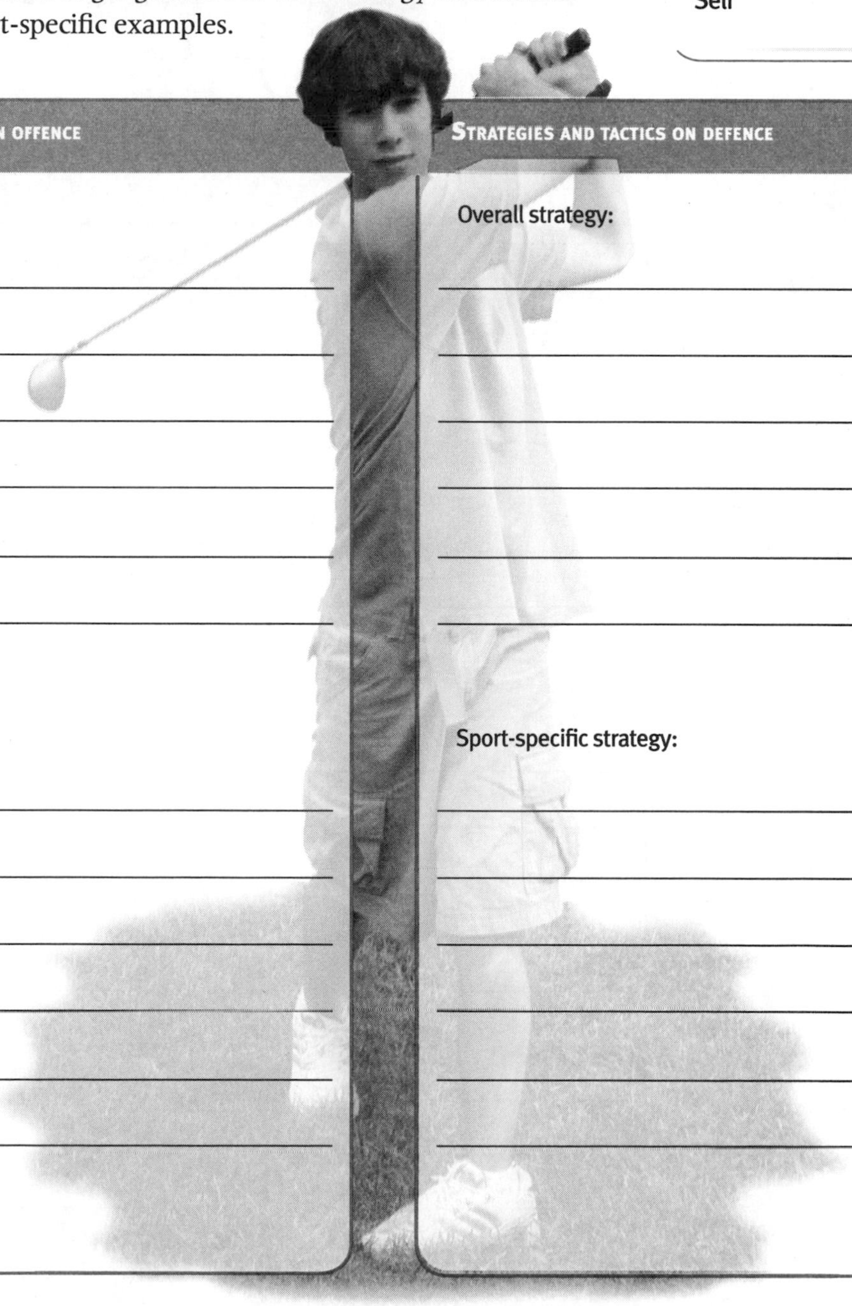

STRATEGIES AND TACTICS ON OFFENCE	STRATEGIES AND TACTICS ON DEFENCE
Overall strategy:	Overall strategy:
Sport-specific strategy:	Sport-specific strategy:

Phases of a Skill

Mission: Choose a skill from one of the target games covered in this chapter. Identify some key points involved in the preparation, execution, and follow-through of this skill and record them on the chart below. Use the "Yes" and "No" columns for self-evaluation, or evaluation by a peer or teacher.

Assessed by:

SPORT	NAME		
	SKILL	YES	NO
Preparation		☐	☐
		☐	☐
		☐	☐
		☐	☐
		☐	☐
		☐	☐
		☐	☐
		☐	☐
Execution		☐	☐
		☐	☐
		☐	☐
		☐	☐
		☐	☐
		☐	☐
		☐	☐
		☐	☐
Follow-Through		☐	☐
		☐	☐
		☐	☐
		☐	☐
		☐	☐
		☐	☐
		☐	☐

ACT High School CPR Student Manual
(Supplementary Material)

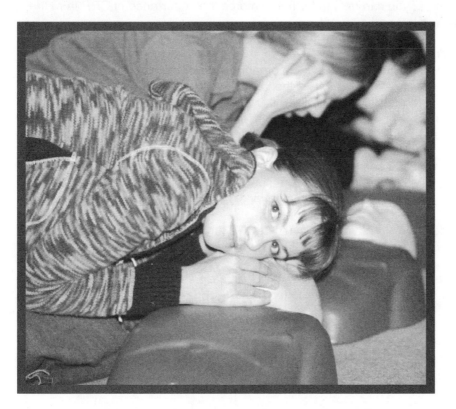

ACT FOUNDATION

CORE PARTNERS:

AstraZeneca
Bristol-Myers Squibb Canada
Pfizer Canada
sanofi-aventis

PROVINCIAL PROGRAM PARTNERS:

Government of Ontario
Hydro One
The Ontario Trillium Foundation
Shoppers Drug Mart

PARENT INFORMATION AND VOLUNTEER LETTER:

Dear Parent/Guardian,

Your teen will learn CPR this school year. This is really important because eight in 10 cardiac arrests occur at home. The good news is that research shows a person's chances of survival can increase by almost four times when a bystander performs CPR.

We are teaching students cardiopulmonary resuscitation (CPR) through the ACT High School CPR Program as part of the curriculum. We will be teaching your teen how to save a life.

Learning CPR in high school empowers youth to help as first responders in an emergency by becoming the first link in the Chain of Survival™, a concept developed by the Heart and Stroke Foundation of Canada that identifies the sequence of events that need to occur to give the victim of a cardiac emergency the best chance of survival. The ACT High School CPR Program will teach students the 4 Rs of CPR: **RISK** factors for heart disease and stroke and the importance of a heart healthy lifestyle; how to **RECOGNIZE** the warning signs of a heart attack, stroke or other developing emergency; how to **REACT**; and finally, the hands-on skill of **RESUSCITATION**.

If you have some expertise as a CPR Instructor, paramedic, firefighter, nurse, doctor or police officer and would like to volunteer some time in the classroom, please contact me at _____.
By assisting us in teaching this course, you can help to further reinforce the importance of CPR from the perspective of both a community member and a parent.

About the ACT High School CPR Program

The ACT Foundation is an award-winning, national charitable organization dedicated to promoting health and empowering Canadians to save lives. ACT establishes the lifesaving CPR program in high schools across Canada so that all youth will graduate with the skills and knowledge to save lives. ACT fundraises for mannequins for schools and guides schools in program set up. Mannequins are donated to schools and high school teachers are trained to teach CPR to students as a regular part of the curriculum. The program would not be possible without the strong support of ACT's program partners, many of which come from our very own community. Ask to see your teen's Student Manual (remember - the information in there is important for you too!) and you will see a list of community partners who have brought this lifesaving program to our school by donating mannequins and providing other support.

Over 900,000 youth across Canada have already been trained in CPR through the ACT program and the results speak for themselves. Students are helping to save lives by calling 9-1-1, helping someone who is choking, or administering CPR. All rescuers are recognized through ACT's **Lifesaver Awards Program**. If your teen uses any of the skills learned through this program to help save a life, please contact ACT by phone, toll free at **1-800-465-9111** or through their Web site (**www.actfoundation.ca**).

We are pleased to teach your teen CPR through the ACT High School CPR Program, but remember it's a skill that's important for you to learn too. Think about it - if you were faced with an emergency situation, wouldn't you want to know what to do? Contact your local CPR agency to learn CPR! To find out where you can learn CPR, visit ACT's Web site.

Sincerely,

_____

Teacher

The ACT Foundation is an award-winning national charitable organization dedicated to promoting health and empowering Canadians to save lives.

ACT's corporate health partners are companies in the research-based pharmaceutical industry:
AstraZeneca, Bristol-Myers Squibb Canada, Pfizer Canada and sanofi-aventis.

EMERGENCY CARE SCENARIOS

Read the following task cards and decide how you would react in each situation. You can respond in writing, act out the scenario, or brainstorm solutions in small groups.

You can also create your own scenario. Use articles from your local newspaper, or think about situations that could take place at home, at school, during a sports event, or at the mall.

✂

1. It is lunch time and all the students pile into the cafeteria. You grab a table with all your friends. You are sitting around the table eating, talking and drinking. Suddenly, Jane clutches her throat. She is not speaking, but her lips begin to turn blue. What do you do?

✂

2. You are walking past your neighbour's house on a warm summer day. Suddenly, you hear your neighbour frantically shouting that her son has fallen into the backyard pool. He can't swim. When you reach the pool deck, you see his body beneath the surface. He is not moving. You are able to reach him and get him out of the pool, but he is unconscious. What do you do?

✂

3. An elderly gentleman is sitting on a park bench. He begins to complain of chest pain. He says he has had it before. As you consider what to do next, you realize that his pain is increasing. What do you do?

✂

4. You are visiting your grandmother's house for lunch. She has just gone into the kitchen. Suddenly, you hear a loud thud. Upon entering the kitchen you see your grandmother on the floor. Her face seems to be drooping somewhat on the left side and she seems unable to move the left side of her body. What do you do?

✂

5. A middle-aged fan at a hockey game has been very excited throughout the match. After the opposition scores the go-ahead goal, he becomes extremely angry, shouting at the referee that the play was offside. In mid-shout he stops, clutching his left arm. He sits down and seems to be having difficulty breathing. He says it feels as though someone is standing on his chest. What do you do?

✂

6. Your uncle is visiting for the holidays. You awake in the night to hear him walking around downstairs. When you go to see him, he complains of indigestion. You recall that he ate his evening meal very early and had nothing to eat later in evening. He is very pale and he appears to be short of breath. What do you do?

✂

7. You are driving on a back road just after a thunderstorm. Up ahead you see a power line down. As you get closer, you see the body of a young woman lying close to the downed line. She is not moving. What do you do?

✂

8. While playing in the gym, Elizabeth starts coughing very hard and leaves the gym to go into the change room. Knowing that Elizabeth always chews gum, what do you do?

PERFORMANCE CHECKLIST - ONE-PERSON CPR (ADULT)

The chart below will help you prepare for your CPR evaluation. Use the checklist to practice before the test with a self-assessment, or an assessment by a classmate. Your teacher will use the rubric on the following page to evaluate your final performance.

OUTCOME	INDICATORS	CHECK
1. For Conscious Casualty Emergency		
Scene Management "Recognize - React"	• Check for hazards, identify yourself and ask for permission to help	❑
	• Assess responsiveness	❑
	• Call for help, call 9-1-1	❑
	• PLT – position, loosen clothing, talk	❑
	• Prepare for ambulance	❑
2. For Unconscious Casualty – Not Breathing		
"React - Resuscitate" (CPR)	• Check for hazards	❑
	• Assess responsiveness	❑
	• Call for help, call 9-1-1	❑
• Open airway	• Head-tilt chin-lift	❑
• Assess breathing	• Assess breathing	❑
• Ventilate	• Ventilate 2 x, watch chest	❑
• Chest compressions and ventilations	• Begin chest compressions	❑
	• Landmark for each compression cycle	❑
	• Compress/release – count	❑
	• Cycle - 30 compressions and 2 breaths (1 second for each breath)	❑
• Continue CPR	• Continue CPR until someone brings an AED, the person moves, or EMS personnel take over	❑

Student name: _____   Assessed by: _____

Class/Period: _____   Teacher ☐

Date: _____   Peer ☐

Self ☐

SAMPLE PERFORMANCE RUBRIC – CPR

Categories	Level 1 (50-59%)	Level 2 (60-69%)	Level 3 (70-79%)	Level 4 (80-100%)
Thinking / Inquiry:	Students will: • with assistance, assess simulated emergency situations • demonstrate they would call 9-1-1 in an emergency situation through role play	Students will: • with some assistance, assess simulated emergency situations and carry out procedures to obtain emergency help	Students will: • usually assess simulated emergency situations and carry out procedures to obtain emergency help	Students will: • independently and with consistency assess simulated emergency situations and demonstrate appropriate emergency response
Applications:	• with direction, carry out basic steps to provide early emergency response for casualty of simulated cardiopulmonary emergency (e.g. heart attack, cardiac arrest, choking) • call 9-1-1 in a simulated emergency situation	• with some assistance, carry out procedures to provide early emergency response for casualty of specific simulated cardiopulmonary emergency (e.g. heart attack, cardiac arrest, choking)	• independently apply procedures to provide early emergency response for casualties of simulated cardiopulmonary emergencies (e.g. heart attack, cardiac arrest, choking)	• fluidly and confidently carry out procedures to assess and provide early emergency response for casualties of simulated cardiopulmonary emergencies

Knowledge & Understanding:	• with assistance make connections between personal behavior and cardiac risk factors and emergencies
	
	• demonstrate a limited understanding of:
	  - their role in the "Chain of Survival"
	  - the anatomy and terminology related to heart problems and heart health
	  - the risk factors related to heart disease
	  - the signs and symptoms of a cardiopulmonary emergency
	  - lifestyle choices to lessen risk
	
	• rarely demonstrate the application of theory to real life situations
		• begin to make connections between personal behavior and cardiac risk factors and emergencies
		
		• demonstrate some understanding of:
		  - their role in the "Chain of Survival"
		  - the anatomy and terminology related to heart problems and heart health
		  - the risk factors related to heart disease
		  - the signs and symptoms of a cardiopulmonary emergency
		  - lifestyle choices to lessen risk
		
		• sometimes apply their theoretical knowledge to real life situations
			• make connections between personal behavior and cardiac risk factors and emergencies
			
			• frequently demonstrate an understanding of most of the concepts related to:
			  - their role in the "Chain of Survival"
			  - the anatomy and terminology related to heart problems and heart health
			  - risk factors that influence heart health
			  - the signs and symptoms of a cardiopulmonary emergency
			  - lifestyle choices to lessen risk
			
			• frequently apply their theoretical knowledge to real life situations
				• make connections between personal and extended family behavior and cardiac risk factors and emergencies
				
				• consistently demonstrate an understanding of:
				  - their role in the "Chain of Survival"
				  - the anatomy and terminology related to heart problems and heart health
				  - how certain lifestyle choices increase or decrease the risk of heart disease
				  - the signs and symptoms of cardiopulmonary emergencies
				  - lifestyle choices to lessen risk
				
				• routinely demonstrate and can explain how theory is applied to real life situations

⋀ACT THE ACT HIGH SCHOOL CPR PROGRAM

Student Evaluation of the CPR Program

CONGRATULATIONS! You have just finished learning the skills of CPR within your physical education class. We would like to ask you some questions about the training so we can continue to make the program better. Please take a few minutes and answer the questions below. **Your answers will be kept confidential.** *Please circle the number that best reflects your opinion on the scale beside each statement. Return the completed questionnaire to your teacher.*

PART A						
Statement	*Strongly disagree*		*Neutral*		*Strongly agree*	
1. The classroom lectures were an important part of the training.	1	2	3	4	5	
2. The information presented in the classroom lectures was easy to understand.	1	2	3	4	5	
3. The student manual was an important part of the training.	1	2	3	4	5	
4. Learning CPR is easy.	1	2	3	4	5	
5. I had enough time to practice with the mannequins.	1	2	3	4	5	
6. My teacher seemed to know a lot about CPR.	1	2	3	4	5	
7. CPR training should be part of the regular school program.	1	2	3	4	5	
8. After taking this course, I think I could do CPR in an emergency situation.	1	2	3	4	5	
9. I think my grade is the right time to learn CPR.	1	2	3	4	5	

PART B			
a) Does anyone in your family have a heart problem?	Yes	No	Unsure
b) Have you ever taken CPR training before?	Yes	No	Unsure
c) Have you ever witnessed anyone having a heart attack in real life?	Yes	No	Unsure
d) Have you spoken with your parents or guardian about any of the information you learned in the CPR course?	Yes	No	Unsure
e) Would you like the CPR course to provide additional heart health information for you and your family?	Yes	No	Unsure
f) As a result of taking the CPR program, are you considering any changes to your lifestyle to become more "heart healthy"?	Yes	No	Unsure

If you've answered "Yes," what heart healthy lifestyle changes are you considering making? _____
_____
_____
_____

g) We are interested in knowing what you thought of the CPR course. Please write your comments below.
_____
_____
_____

School Board/Division: _____   Grade Level: _____   Male ❑   Female ❑

School: _____   Date: _____

Community: _____

LIFESAVER AWARDS PROGRAM–FEEDBACK FORM

Feedback on rescues involving students following their training is important for all of us to hear about. Please ask your students if they have used any of their CPR skills and knowledge to help save a life. Whether it is calling 9-1-1, performing the Heimlich Manoeuvre, or CPR, we want to hear about it.

STUDENT INFORMATION:

Last name: _____   First name: _____

Grade: _____   School: _____

School Board: _____   Teacher: _____

Date of Rescue (If you can't recall, please indicate month/year or season/year): _____

Community: _____

HOW YOU HELPED:

Please note on the list below, in what ways you have applied your knowledge from your CPR course in a real life situation.

❑ Recognizing the warning signs of a heart attack and helping a person seek medical help (calling 911)

❑ CPR

❑ Airway Obstruction Manoeuvre (helping someone who is choking)

❑ Helping in another type of emergency. Please explain below.

WHAT HAPPENED?

Please describe the "who, what, where and when" of what happened.

_____
_____
_____
_____
_____
_____

Age (approximate) and gender of person you helped:

Age: _____   ☐ Male   ☐ Female

**Please return this form to the ACT Foundation by fax: (613) 729-5837,
by mail: 379 Holland Avenue, Ottawa, ON K1Y 0Y9, or call us at 1-800-465-9111.**

Notes:

Notes:

Notes:

Notes: